Why Am I
HERE?

Why Am I
H E R E ?

A Concise Guide to Your
Purpose and Potential

JOYCE KELLER
with ELAINE J. KELLER

4th Dimension Press • Virginia Beach • Virginia

To Jack, Elaine, Scott, Alex, John, Nick, Flo, and Tina.
The great loves of my life.

*The two most important days in your life are the
day you are born and the day you find out why.*
Mark Twain

*Occasionally I told astrologers to select my worst periods, according to
planetary indications, and I would still accomplish whatever task I set
myself. It is true that my success at times has been preceded by extraordinary
difficulties. But my conviction has always been justified: faith in the divine
protection, and the right use of man's God-given will, are forces formidable
beyond any the "inverted bowl" can muster. The starry inscription at one's
birth, I came to understand, is not that man is a puppet of his past. Its
message is rather a prod to pride; the very heavens seek to arouse man's
determination to be free from every limitation. God created each man as a
soul, dowered with individuality, hence essential to the universal structure,
whether in the temporary role of pillar or parasite. His freedom is final and
immediate, if he so wills; it depends not on outer but inner victories.*
Paramahansa Yogananda, *Autobiography of a Yogi*

Contents

Acknowledgments

To Elaine Keller, a great author and friend, who wrote *Karmascopes*, and to my wonderful support system at A.R.E. Press. I love all of you.

Introduction

What is Karma, Really?

You've heard of "karma," of course. By now, nearly everyone has. In fact, we've been pretty much deluged by self-help gurus theorizing on the subject, so much so that phrases like "instant karma," "it must be karmic," "good karma," and "bad karma," have invaded our vocabulary, seeming to threaten either perpetual doom or good luck by an unknown and a grossly unfair set of gods.

The fact is that karma is a centuries-old school of thought linked to the Eastern concept of reincarnation. Reincarnation's basis is that through each rebirth we are given new opportunities to develop ourselves and alter past mistakes by changing the *attitudes* associated with making these mistakes. Not changing the underlying attitudes causes a worsening set of circumstances, and as we undergo increasingly difficult experiences, we seem to be caught in the grip of a relentless downward spiral. But this is not cause for worry. The purpose of these bad or unpleasant experiences is to bring about a positive change in our temperament, leading to our soul's evolution. Someone who wantonly takes life for granted without regard for the pain and suffering of others, for example, may find himself in a situation that elicits his compassion for others while providing the opportunity for him to experience the sacredness of life. That's what karma is—an *opportunity*.

For this reason we select our own experiences prior to birth—yes, we select our situations!—and these experiences become opportunities for growth. Likewise, our astrological chart is preselected with our highest good in mind, put into place for us to best experience spiritual progression. Nothing about our births is arbitrary, but instead consists of a design created to set into motion our one constant and greatest gift, the meter by which all our decisions are made on earth: that of free will. Free will is the motor that propels us forward with the assistance of our moral compass, spiritual rudder, and sense of discernment.

Helping us along the way to evolution is *inner knowledge*, knowing ourselves and the meaning of the pitfalls we face, so as to best dodge them and create a blissful, caring, and fulfilled life.

You may be asking, with so many how-to-succeed books offering creative visualization, positive thinking, and success affirmations, why do so few succeed at creating a beautiful life for themselves, filled with all the good things humans yearn for, such as success in career, family relationships, and love?

Many of the self-help gurus today have obviously read up on karma. While they have gotten some of it right, many have missed the point by focusing on karmic causes in this lifetime. In truth, karma is brought about by *past life* attitudes that need to be corrected before we can succeed in the present.

The other misconception is in not understanding another great truth: karma is *changeable*. This misunderstanding has given the karmic principle a ring of finality, ignoring the power within each of us that is capable of influencing and changing our life direction and experiences. This is why we have been given free will. Karma is not to be suffered through like some harsh penance or punishment; rather, karma is intended to be transformational. Our karma is influenced by our every step through life, shaped by our growing attitude and understanding, and can be washed away just as the waves wash away our footsteps in the sand.

So, the missing part of the equation involves the personal karma of the individual, and his or her freely-chosen actions and attitudes that can change it.

More than half of our current life problems stem from past-life actions. This is the first key to take into account on your journey to life improvement.

The Karmic Doctrine and Past-Life Hold-Overs

The Karmic Doctrine is a spiritual law that is meant to keep us moving toward greater development of our individual soul–the link to our consciousness and individuality that survives physical death. This doctrine carries forward from lifetime to lifetime and through the non–physical in–between periods as well as those in the third dimension here on earth. If we touch a hot stove, we instantly react by jerking back our finger, learning to never do that again. There are thoughtless, ignorant, ill–advised, inconsiderate, mean, or evil acts committed by those who do not appear to undergo an instantaneous reaction or learning experience. We see people doing terribly bad things in their lives while living out their days in comfort and wealth. We wonder why there is no justice and how the universe could let this happen.

This is where the Karmic Doctrine comes in. It is a law that balances our actions and attitudes and carries over from one physical lifetime to another, or sometimes several. It turns the tables and subjects us to the same or similar conditions we imposed or wished on another in a past life. These conditions are not meant to punish but to enhance our understanding through experiencing what the other person or people went through as a result of our actions, or lack of action. Soul memories from a past life, lying deep in our subconscious, affect us in our current lifetime through emotions. Past–life experiences become part of our emotional makeup in a new lifetime. Strong likes, dislikes, fears, and phobias in this life are usually due to subconscious memories of our experiences from a past life.

Deep within our consciousness, these hidden memories affect us greatly, sometimes in negative or restrictive ways. Many people have been helped through hypnosis, by means of past–life regression techniques, to eliminate these past–life memories that are causing problems for them in their current life. But hypnosis is not a requisite for accessing this information, as you will see. This book relays my method for getting to this hidden wisdom and will provide you with the necessary tools to understand where you have been in the past and how these experiences may be affecting you now. I say "may" be affecting you, because each individual is different and is in a unique phase of his evolutionary path. As always, you are meant to use your powers of discernment to decide how much of the following information applies to you in the here and now, and to use what does apply to your soul's highest advantage.

Our subconscious is aware of what we need for our growth. We select an easy or a hard path, the hardest being the most accelerated type of development; the easiest, the most outwardly enjoyable but slowest in its spiritual rewards. Though we inwardly know the meaning of our lessons, their purpose has too often become obscured by our needs, wants, and the disconnection of day-to-day life. When our personal karma is understood, and altered, life becomes renewing and forgiving. The weight is lifted. That is what this book is designed to help you do: lift the weight you may be feeling, and remove the obstacles blocking your personal happiness and evolutionary path.

This part of the Karmic Doctrine, taught by the Eastern religions of Buddhism and Hinduism, was brought into the Western consciousness in the early twentieth century by the amazing "sleeping prophet," Edgar Cayce. Between the years 1901 and 1945, Cayce, a devout Christian, gave more than 14,000 psychic readings in a trance-like sleep state. Of those, the life readings, or "life histories," as he called them, delved into past lives and brought to light a range of concepts, including karma and reincarnation. This was the first time many Westerners heard of these terms.

In *Many Mansions: The Edgar Cayce Story of Reincarnation*, author Gina Cerminara explains: "No matter what our difficulty . . . we must realize that only through the transformation of the self can the situation be transcended. Our own attitudes must be changed; our own conduct must be altered. Attitudes cannot be critical, condemnatory, vengeful, proud, indifferent, negative; conduct cannot be selfish, inconsiderate, unsocial."

Karma is the law of *cause and effect*. "What ye sow, so shall ye reap." In other words, what you give out, you will get back. It knows no time or limitations, pushing forth the evolutionary path of the soul as it moves toward its final and highest destination of enlightenment, self-realization, or "godliness." Karma acts on a subliminal and spiritual level, affecting us physically and emotionally. If we do not know why we experience what we do, it is because our subconscious memories don't usually hold the awareness of thoughts, intentions, or actions of former lifetimes affecting our existence in the here and now.

Karma does not link us up with spiritual memory, however. We may experience a balancing or growth opportunity without understanding why we are confronted with this particular lesson. This is because it would be traumatizing for us to see the actual causes of our current path, and so it is with divine grace that we are spared this knowledge. Our conscious memory of past–life experience is blocked out by a shield of protection, linking us up only with those memories we need to understand in order to keep from repeating the same mistakes.

For this reconnection with spiritual memory, I use the tool of astrology. While astrological horoscopes found online or in the daily paper paint with a broad brush that often only applies to the individual in a general way, I have, through my years of practice, fine–tuned my understanding of planetary placement, in order to ascertain where we've come from, and what we are supposed to be learning from it. In other words, to understand not only our soul's past, but our soul's potential.

Why Am I Here? is about reconnection with our higher selves. It is about new understanding and growth, while penetrating the protective shield that links us with, and at the same time protects us from, the memories and experiences that lie at the root of our current problems and situations. This book will help you cut through the veil and supply answers without causing trauma in the process.

This book also explains what the causes of our heartaches, problems, or confusions might be. These summaries are not meant to generate guilt, but to encourage analysis and introspection. It's up to you to turn to your own inner guidance to ascertain what applies to yourself and what doesn't. Only your heart and inner mind can reveal this to you.

It is no more surprising to be born twice than it is to be born once.
—Voltaire

Attaining "Moksha," or Soul Liberation

According to the Hindu religion, the purpose and destiny of all souls on the earth is "moksha," or soul liberation. It is freedom from rebirth on the physical plane. Our soul then continues to evolve in the astral plane known as "Antariksa," until there is the final stage–the merging with Siva, or the Godhead. It is then like water returning to the sea–a sea of bliss.

Moksha comes when earthly karma has been resolved, and humans are fully God-realized. There cannot be any deeds left undone, anyone to forgive, or any further necessary Earth experience. If any of this is left undone, we can be pulled back into earthly expression and birth. As taught by Sri Paramahansa Yogananda, all souls ultimately strive for self-realization. That is the reason his organization, Self-Realization Fellowship (SRF), in Los Angeles, Calif., thrives, to this day. It is considered by many to be the gateway to soul liberation.

Soul liberation often unfolds when there is tremendous generosity–generosity that involves giving, and then giving even more, until it is impossible to continue giving. Being able to give generously may be the ultimate test of soul development and ultimate soul liberation–liberation that ends the seemingly endless cycle of earthly incarnations. Saying, "I don't want to be born here again," may or may not qualify a person for Moksha, the ending of their cycle of reincarnation.

When a seeker has unfolded to the point where he wants to end the cycle of earthly experiences, the desire for giving to others becomes increasingly powerful and spontaneous. He or she will always be looking for an opportunity to do something good for someone else. When someone has not unfolded into this pattern of generosity, he thinks about himself a great deal, and he calculates his generosity in proportion to what he will receive, or by something else. By giving in proportion to what will be received, he is creating future limitations. He is saying, "I am just this big, and I will always be just this size, because that is as far as my consciousness can take me." Karma doesn't work that way. Human consciousness is not like that, because by limiting or calculating your generosity, you are shrinking your consciousness, rather than expanding it to divine love and experience. It will cause pulling away from God, rather than reconnection.

If your heart is full of joy, you will be more confident, and have more to give to others. Another secret of soul growth is to have little or no awareness of what is given away to others. Give freely and generously, without calculating the value of the gift. Do not remember your generosity. Do not wait for or expect a return for your acts of generosity.

Give freely, and then, let it quickly be forgotten. Why do we have to remember, when there are universal soul records that know everything?

Is There Such a Thing as Good Karma and Bad Karma?

The following is from the Vedic Scriptures on karma, *Dancing with Siva*:

> In the highest sense, there is no good or bad karma. All experience offers opportunities for spiritual growth. Selfless, kind acts yield positive, uplifting conditions. Selfish acts yield conditions of negativity and confusion.
>
> Karma itself is neither good nor bad, but a neutral principle that governs energy and motion of thought, word, and deed. All experiences help us grow. Good, loving actions bring us lovingness through others. Mean, selfish acts return to us pain and suffering. Kindness produces sweet fruits, called, "punya." Unkindness yields spoiled fruits, called, "papa." As we mature, life after life, we go through much pain and joy. Actions that are in tune with our destiny, or dharma, help us along the path, while wrong actions impede or slow down our progress. The divine law is that whatever karma we are experiencing in our life is just what we need at the moment, and nothing can happen but that we have the strength to meet it. Even harsh karma, when faced with wisdom, can be the greatest catalyst for spiritual enfoldment. Performing daily tasks, keeping good company, going to holy places, seeing to others' needs—all evoke the higher energies, direct the mind to useful thoughts, and avoid the creation of troublesome new karma. The Vedas explain, "According as one behaves, so does he become. One becomes virtuous by virtuous action, bad by bad action.

During my life, I have had the good fortune to work with a masterful group of teachers and angels who come through to me in meditation, dreams, automatic writing, whenever I am driving a car–one of my most receptive times–or while I am channeling. They come whenever I need an answer or redirection, or to offer insight. *Why Am I Here?* is the offspring of this information.

I have come to know some of my guides extremely well, particularly those who have been with me through my entire life. One of these is Babaji, who in Hinduism is revered as the Father. To me he is a patient and very blessed teacher. Babaji first appeared at my bedside when I was four years old, looking remarkably like Santa Claus with a dark tan. Through Babaji and his equally holy sister, and feminine counterpart, Mataji, I was carefully, but pointedly, guided to the world beyond conventional Western thought.

Other guides come and go for different purposes, and some, I have learned, have been with me over many lifetimes. Of these, I have had particular influence from members of the Self-Realization Fellowship. This organization, with which Babaji and Mataji are fundamentally involved, is written about extensively by its founder, Paramahansa Yogananda, in his extraordinary book *Autobiography of a Yogi*. The principle tenet of self-realization is that the purpose of life is evolution. This is accomplished through self-effort, says Yogananda, and through "lifting of man's limited mortal consciousness into God Consciousness." Self-realization is the knowledge that "we share kinship with God, and possess a superiority of mind over body, and soul over mind."

Through my work with master teachers, life-work with individuals on clairvoyant or intuitive levels, and through my own readings, I have become convinced of these and other spiritual truths. Many of these are offered in *Why Am I Here?* in the hopes that they will be of interest and service to you.

Part I

How It All
Relates to You

I consider myself a Hindu, Christian,
Muslim, Jew, Buddhist, and Confucian.
Mahatma Gandhi

CHAPTER 1

The Tip of the Iceberg

The System

If you are reading this book, it's pretty clear by now that you must have wondered at least once whether you've lived in another time and, if so, who you were. Maybe you have wondered if, and *how*, those past lives are affecting your present life. Have you also wondered about being instantly attracted to a special person, knowing on some level that you have not only met before, but might even be *soul mates*? Do you have recurring money issues and wonder whether these problems are part of some pattern set in place even before you were born? Do you play music by ear without any training and wonder how? Do you have a special affinity for languages? Do you know a prodigy? All of these, I have come to learn, are indications of past–life issues, tendencies, and relationships, as well as karma that has been left unfinished. My intention is for this book to help you bring these issues out into the open, and achieve a successful and fulfilling resolution, once and for all.

Why Am I Here? offers a simple system to unlock the secrets of your past lives and their impact on your present life. It's not your imagination when you feel you "know" that teller at the bank, or that you dislike your neighbor upon first sight; you may very well have had negative interactions with this person in a recent lifetime.

This book will tell you:
- What you were like in your past life
- Why you were born
- Where you are going with your life

- What you should be doing with your life
- Who your soul mate might be
- Your greatest financial success
- Your best career path
- The karmic issues you are tangling with

Why Am I Here? also contains:

My one-of-a-kind Karmic Dictionary, which you can use to pinpoint the underlying emotional cause behind a particular issue.

Why Am I Here reveals my tried-and-true technique to find your soul mate and stay together, and how to attain the fulfillment and lasting abundance you strive for. It will help you discover the life contract that you agreed to prior to your birth, and to become what you are meant to be—fulfilling your most deeply held dreams and potential.

Why Am I Here? does this by taking an obscure but amazingly helpful technique of reading the "Nodes" of the moon (from your astrology chart), and turning this information into a workable system meant to improve your life.

Ancient metaphysicians realized that the position of the "South Node" in a person's birth chart indicated his most recent past incarnations and experiences. In my own work, I came to realize that this signal could be used as a means of unlocking the mystery of where that person had been, and what attitudes he might be carrying over. I refer to this "carry-over" as the *soul memory*.

The metaphysicians also discovered that the "North Node" indicates the most important lessons, experiences, and relationships a person may experience in their current lifetime. I refer to these promising possibilities as the *soul potential*.

Why Am I Here? helps you quickly access this information, then apply it in the most creative, effective way possible.

> There is nothing noble to being superior to some other man. The true nobility is being superior to your previous self.—Hindu Proverb

Unlocking Your Karma

Why Am I Here? offers a simple, easy-to-understand system for discovering and correcting your karma.

In my twenty-odd years as an on-air psychic on America's longest-running New Age live, call-in radio show, I've developed a system of tuning into and correcting life's problems. I have put this system into practice not only in my own shows and books, but on *The Morning Show with Regis Philbin*, on *Oprah, Entertainment Tonight*, and in countless other public forums.

The system is easy and begins with "unlocking" your karma. To do this, my system isolates certain aspects of our individual makeup, including personality trends, why we're here, and where we've come from.

The Keys

You'll see that unlocking, or advancing, one's karma is not difficult if you understand the keys.

Where Is Your Personality Taking You?

The first key is uncovering your basic make-up. These are your character traits, or the way you address the situations in life. The personality has the ability to move us in either a negative or a positive direction, which are both pointed out here.

Where Have You Come from?

The second key is uncovering where you've come from. *The Soul Memory Tables* indicate why you have been born in the present, and what your lesson is.

What Is Your Potential?

The third key is uncovering why you're here, or the purpose of your birth. This is what you're here to do now to get rid of karmic indebtedness incurred in the past.

The Soul Potential Tables give an indication of current life lessons, health, money, success issues, and soul mates.

Initiate the Karmic Shift

The fourth key is initiating the Karmic Shift, or the awakening of a new outlook, by recognizing the situations that are in place for our growth. *The Challenges List* helps identify these situations.

Remove Harmful Attitudes

The fifth key is isolating underlying attitudes perpetuating problems and issues in your life by using the *Attitudes, Conditions, and Tendencies* list.

Change Your Emotional Condition

The sixth key is to discern where your underlying attitudes are taking you. The *Karmic Dictionary* is arranged alphabetically for easy reference, and allows you to look up the meaning of difficulties as they arise.

Apply the Lessons of Your Life

The seventh key: use this meaning, or underlying emotional condition, to implement your *Life Lessons*.

Follow your road with understanding, discernment, and an open heart, and see where it takes you. Don't be surprised if it takes you where you want to go.

> **As above, so below**
> **We are all one**
> **God is in all of us, and in all things.**
> **—Anonymous**

Religions on Reincarnation

Buddhism: Incarnations are caused by karma and earthly cravings that must be overcome in the pursuit of spiritual perfection. Liberation from rebirth is achieved when one overcomes the "three unwholesome roots": desire, hatred, and delusion—and attains nirvana, or enlightenment, a state of ineffable peace.

Christianity: While early versions of the Bible confirm the theory of reincarnation, no mainstream Christian denomination officially supports the concept.

Hinduism: Reincarnation is caused by imperfections of the soul; ignorance and desire perpetuate the need to reincarnate. The soul perfects itself by purifying and realizing itself, shedding earthly desires.
Islam: The Koran: "He brings back to life the dead earth, similarly ye shall be reborn."
Judaism: The early Jews believed in transmigration, or the passage of a soul upon death into another body. —Rosemary Ellen Guiley, *Harper's Encyclopedia of Mystical and Paranormal Experience*

CHAPTER 2

The Life of the Soul

Our Ultimate Purpose

I was a teenager when I first got my driver's license. My mother saw that as an opportunity for me to deliver to my dad anything he might have forgotten to take to work, including his lunch, sweater, hat, scarf, or gloves. My dad was the pharmacist at a large mental institution on Long Island in New York, and my mother always admonished, "Don't walk through the wards. Just park outside the pharmacy and please just drop this off to your dad. Don't stop to observe, bond, or talk with the patients!" She knew me so well. She knew that I found this institution and the people it housed fascinating. I would park far away from the Pharmacy Department, and enter through any doors that might have been left open. Sometimes, I found myself walking through wards where the patients were heavily drugged and in a deep-sleep state. They would be sitting around, watching television or playing cards. Some were wandering through the halls. I noticed something very strange about many of the patients. Some were in period costumes. Some women wore flowing robes and gowns. Some had high pointy hats with veils, while others wore crowns, skull caps, and a wide array of odd-looking head gear. The variety of garb was impressive and intriguing. I wanted to know more. Through the years, I thought often about those patients. As I studied metaphysics and learned about the continuation of existence through many physical lives, I came to realize that these people were reliving existences from previous incarnations. I learned that over-indulgence in alcohol or mind-altering drugs can break through our protective shield, or aura. The damaging of the protective veil that separates our present consciousness from our past–life memories can cause a confused state of mind. We all have that electromagnetic shield, or aura, surrounding us. It can be seen by some psychics and can be photographed using Kirlian photography. When this aura is damaged by drinking excessive alcohol, shock treatments, or use of certain drugs, we can enter a reality that is more of a past–life memory than the present. We can leave ourselves open to the intrusion of disincarnate entities that influence our behavior and cause undesirable and dangerous actions. These visits to the state mental hospital had a profound effect on me and contributed greatly to my desire to learn more about our prior lifetimes, and helped begin an intense search for the truth about life and the possibilities created by reincarnation.

The great mystic, Paramahansa Yogananda, said that we would probably go insane if we had clear recall of our past lives. "God, in His grace and infinite wisdom, pulls down the shield that closes off the memories of our prior incarnations." The fact that we may remember past lives in bits and pieces, as some did in the mental institution, fascinated me. I began to look for other ways our previous incarnations crept into our present life, perhaps in ways we were totally unaware.

As I quoted Paramahansa Yogananda earlier in this book, " . . . faith in divine protection, and right use of man's God–given will, are forces more formidable than are influences flowing through the heaven. The starry inscription at one's birth, I came to understand, is not that man is a puppet of his past, its message is rather a prod to pride; the very heavens seek to arouse man's determination to be free of every limitation. God created each man as a soul, dowered with individuality . . . His freedom is final and immediate, if he so wills; it depends not on outer but inner victories." He is stating that while astrology presents a basic pattern, man's unique individuality and free will give him the power to overcome any obstacle that may be in his path, with the result of becoming a pillar of strength, or that of a parasite, completely his own doing.

Nonetheless, I found, the influences present from our past lives can prove to be powerful impediments to our success as individuals, and to the fulfillment of our potential. These influences can create cyclical behavior that hinders us from attaining happiness, fulfillment, and joy. What if, I wondered, we had a way of identifying these past–life influences, and overcoming them?

If you are still stuck on the issue of reincarnation, then I hope you realize that as humans, we are much too profound and complex to have lived only one lifetime. Look at the many instances of child prodigies, or of young people who remember specific incidents, people, or locations from prior lives. How about the many individuals who find they are able to speak languages they have never studied?

As for experiences or actions from previous incarnations that have created karma affecting us now, you may wonder why you should be held responsible for past–life actions that you can't remember. Many people think this is unfair. Why be physically or emotionally challenged, or in some way handicapped in the twenty–first century for mistakes made perhaps hundreds of years before? Who remembers these things? Is each new baby actually carrying eons of lifetimes of experiences into each new incarnation, both good and bad?

Yes, we carry our past deeds in our "soul memory." *The Egyptian Book of the Dead* refers to this soul memory, or soul record, as the Akashic record. If we don't learn the lessons that we should have learned at a certain point in our soul's development, it's possible to accrue and experience "karma." Karma can be rough, but it can also be rewarding. It depends upon the growth of the soul, and your ability to understand, respect, and practice the universal laws.

Balance and harmony of the soul's energy is important. If we become too out–of–balance, perhaps with too many lifetimes of wealth and extravagance, our Higher Intelligence, or the God within, may encourage us to choose a lifetime of poverty and deprivation for the soul's greatest growth experience. I like to call these adjustments "soul tweaking."

We incarnate as male and female, because we must experience and know the nature of being in both a male and female body. The ultimate purpose of reincarnation is soul perfection, and perfect reconnection with our Creator. As we grow in perfection and godliness, we eventually come to the point of being able to truly sit at the right hand of God. At this point of soul perfection, we return to the Source. After that, we are given opportunities to move into even higher realms of existence or to return to the earth for further service.

My mother had a unique way of explaining some of these things.

When I was young, she told me about God's "great big book," and His great big pen that He used to write everyone's name in the book. Everything we did was recorded in that book. Of course, I secretly laughed at this. Now I know that that "big book" is the soul's Akashic record. As I started studying religions of the world, I learned that the Akashic record is the invisible but real record of our soul's activity. This record follows us lifetime to lifetime, and is revealed to us after the time of our physical death in each lifetime. The record is imbedded within the human heart and mind.

Even though we may not consciously remember past lives, every one of our thoughts, words, and deeds are indelibly etched into our soul record, and follow us through each lifetime. Yet there is a subconscious veil that separates the lifetimes so that each one clearly stands on its own. If we remembered all our past lives on a conscious level, we would become extremely confused and quite possibly insane. One lifetime would run into the other without our being able to differentiate our present reality from that of past "fantasies." Each lifetime is confusing enough and just about all that most can people can manage. If we break through the protective mental barrier, which in India is known as "piercing the Bindu," or a Kundalini awakening, we will recall past lives. If done in a gentle, logical way, with an experienced regressionist, these memories can be wonderfully enlightening and amazing.

Over my lifetime of practice as a psychic counselor, I have learned that recalling past lives can be not only eye–opening, but highly therapeutic when used to understand why we experience, and sometimes become stuck on, situations in the present. Past lives can be used to shed light on romantic difficulties, family relationship issues, living up to our career desires, and much more. Paired with astrology, which I have also used to great effect in my career, this knowledge can be used to break negative patterns and help you achieve your highest potential without the need for regression, or hypnosis, or any negative concerns.

This is my own system that I've created and developed. It has been used successfully on thousands of individuals.

Why Am I Here? reveals my system for the first time, in a format you can easily put to use in your life now.

CHAPTER 3

Your Inner Soul

What Is Your Soul, Really?

There's been a lot of discussion about souls, and "inner conscious-ness," and similar–sounding con-cepts, but do we really understand what these ideas mean? The soul is known to be the essence of a human being, the repository of thoughts, memories, stimuli, and dreams. It is the core that animates us, propels us to action, or causes us to hang back and linger. It is the seat of reason and understanding, the fulcrum of our thoughts, words, and deeds.

But this still doesn't fully describe what souls are.

The soul is thought to be indestructible, no matter what fate con-fronts the body or mind that it inhabits.

Buddhism calls the soul the "Greater Self," while the lesser self dis-appears at death. This greater self is the life force, or will to live, that survives successive rebirths. According to Eastern philosophy, the soul pushes forward, ever–evolving, growing, and seeking, unless meeting with stagnation. When a soul stops learning and expanding, it may wither, but it will never die. Knowledge gained through experience is the soul's fuel, and through this it changes and expands, effortlessly or heavily, always probing, and hopefully, always growing. For when we stop learning, we leave this life.

In the phase of our experience we call death, in which we depart one plane of existence and head for another, the soul takes its leave of the body. It may stay around the earth plane for a while; often this is a period of adjustment before it accepts it is no longer "alive" in the earth–

ly sense. After this adjustment it can move on and reunite with those out-of-body beings it has known in the past, and who have assisted and nurtured its development over this, and many, many incarnations.

Once, at the time of creation of man, we were God-like. Through the use of free will, we chose to experience coming into physical bodies for our greater understanding. As we became increasingly stuck in the delights of the flesh—how we like those foods and other physical experiences!—the vibrations of the earth became denser, holding us closer. We eventually lost our ability to come and go as free spirits. We could no longer leave our physical bodies at will and return to the Creator. Thus the pattern of creating Earth karma began, and it became increasingly difficult for us to give up what we enjoyed in the physical. This does not mean we have to give up all our earthly passions and become nuns or monks. It is meant to trigger the awareness that who we are encompasses much more than what is apparent here on Earth's surface. We are also capable of much more than what is apparent. In fact, we are potentially capable of anything.

A majority of the world believes in reincarnation, with a rising number of Americans thinking it might be possible. The purpose of reincarnating perhaps hundreds or thousands of times is soul perfection-godliness-growing to a state of wholeness and understanding, so that we may become complete and rejoin the Creator as co-creators. To do this, we must become completely cognizant of our actions and how they affect other people. You may, as you become more aware, begin to act in a wholly unselfish manner. This does not mean, however that you cannot still enjoy the fruits of the earth. Maybe Earth's fruits are put in place for us to help others and ourselves enjoy, as long as we are not hurting others or ourselves in doing so.

We all are co-creators to some extent at this stage of our evolution, because of the gift of free will. Proceeding through life, we use that free will through each and every choice. As we interact with others and create new karmic situations or work out old karma, we are ever-evolving and growing toward that ideal state of perfection.

No man can reveal to you aught but that which already lies half asleep in the dawning of your knowledge.—Kahlil Gibran

The Temporal Zone

A few weeks after my mother's sudden death, she appeared to me during meditation. During this, the first of many visits, she told me about a place she had visited called the Temporal Zone. This is the holding place for purification, in which the soul is cleansed of the earth's dense vibration before moving on to a higher level. Here, souls are given a period of therapy and rest along with healing waters of rejuvenation. Gently, they are helped to move beyond the travail of Earth. Astral hospitals are available for people who need additional healing—to mollify their trauma or help them to forgive—if they would otherwise be unable to move on.

At any point after reaching the astral, or ethereal, level, the soul is confronted with the karmic implications of the life it left behind. Every word, thought, action, and intention is reviewed. With master teachers, strengths and weaknesses are analyzed, and together a determination is made about the individual's needs. This process occurs within a calendar based on cosmic time, and so may ensue over a period of decades, centuries, or a millennium. With the masters' guidance, lifetimes are reviewed to choose what karma can be worked on. It may be in an accelerated or difficult manner, or more cautious and easy.

Parents who can provide the proper lessons are selected, and to some degree, the individual's experiences for its next incarnation are charted and decided upon.

Only Enlightenment, according to Buddhists, eliminates new karma and the need to reincarnate. The earth is seen as a place of great turmoil, and lifetimes spent here can be difficult and unpleasant. But the earth is also a place of learning, and when the lessons are received and successfully implemented, we may move on. If we choose not to learn or receive, we stay in a place of darkness, and the lessons become harder, more difficult to bear, and occasionally, life–altering.

> The Sleeping Prophet, Edgar Cayce, describes an apparent out-of-body trip to the Akashic Records to get information on a client.
> He said he felt himself leave his body and travel in a narrow, straight shaft of light. . . .
> Finally, he arrived at a hill, where he saw a mount and a great

temple. Inside was a large room like a library, filled with books of people's lives.

All he had to do was pull down the book he wanted.—Hugh Lynn Cayce and Noel Langley, *Edgar Cayce on Reincarnation*

It is nature's kindness that we do not remember past births . . . Life would be a burden if we carried such a tremendous load of memories.—Mahatma Gandhi

CHAPTER 4

Breaking Patterns

Karmic Correction

You know by now that karma is the universal law of cause and effect, or, "What ye sow, so shall ye reap." You also know by now that karma is created by our actions, words, and thoughts, but most importantly, by our intent. Also, you know that there is no such thing as "Good Karma" or "Bad Karma," and that karma is not a punishment. Instead, karmic experiences, which include nearly all our experiences, are for the purpose of balancing, or *karmic correction*. This correction is meant to provide an opportunity for learning, growth, and our eventual rebirth as we head toward the state of God–perfection, and enlightenment.

Understanding karma and its universal laws helps us to straighten out our lives, and to keep to the paths we wish to follow.

> Sometimes the dissonance between reality and false beliefs reaches a point when it becomes impossible to avoid the awareness that the world no longer makes sense. Only then is it possible for the mind to consider radically different ideas and perceptions.
> —Mark Engel, from Gregory Bateson's
> *Steps to an Ecology of Mind*

You may be still questioning these ideas, thinking that the whole "karmic correction" idea is unjust. You may still ask why human beings have to pay off karma that they don't remember creating. Why suffer problems or handicaps in the current century for choices made eons ago?

It is important to know that karmic correction is not necessary if in the soul's evolution through the rebirth process, the individual eliminates the imbalance. The purpose of rebirth is first and always *balance*. The universal law is, that when a part of the soul's development is lacking or overabundant, the situation requires correction. For example, several lives of affluence may call for lifetimes of poverty, especially if greed or lack of compassion for those less fortunate manifests in one's nature. So too, many lifetimes as one sex may cause a lack of empathy for the other. So we incarnate as the other sex, until there is balance, appreciation, and understanding of the natures of both male and female.

The Akashic Records

Although we may not consciously remember past lives, every one of our thoughts, words, and deeds is indelibly etched into the journals of our soul. These journals are known as the Akashic Records, the knowledge of which is contained in the ethers, or surrounding atmosphere. This knowledge is also contained within *seed atoms*, etheric kernels of knowledge which circulate within our beings and remain with us from lifetime to lifetime.

It is through God's grace that we do not consciously remember past lives. We cannot work on the unfinished karma of our present existence while weighted down with recall of other lives. A person cannot function within the reality of 21st century America, for example, and the intricacies peculiar to this time frame and his/her own individuality, if he/she is simultaneously experiencing a set of experiences belonging to a different place and existence. It is just too confusing. The conflict and chaos it would create would keep us from properly proceeding in this incarnation.

The memories of actions engendered by previous incarnations do not belong in the present. It is enough that we carry the emotions, if they are strong enough to remain with us, and the subconscious recollection of these circumstances. An abundant conscious memory can not only be confusing, but can manifest in guilt, phobias, and illness. For instance, someone who murdered his spouse in a past life may be reunited with her in this lifetime in order to learn unconditional love, compassion for suffering, and forgiveness. Yet he would not be able to proceed if plagued with overt recall of his past deed. He would not be able to love her the way he was supposed to in order to be wounded by her transgressions, nor be able to learn how to forgive. He would excuse her if hampered by the knowledge of his past deeds. He would believe that her actions were his own doing, and would never learn unconditional love. He would probably proceed in misery, saddled with guilt, confusion, and trauma. In due time, these emotions would more than likely create instability, illness, and inappropriate behavior.

While all incarnations are not necessarily so dramatic, the present must proceed on its own, with knowledge of previous lives occurring gradually, when the person can understand and accept them into his consciousness. Our angels and guides are here to help us and will see that we receive this information if and when we are ready. We will know that it is appropriate to accept these experiences because of their positive effect, and by the feelings of enlightenment and liberation they generate.

> I read about an Eskimo hunter who asked the local missionary priest, "If I did not know about God and sin would I go to hell?"
> "No," said the priest, "not if you did not know."
> "Then why," asked the Eskimo earnestly, "did you tell me?"
> —Annie Dillard

> He shall give his angels charge over thee to keep thee in all His ways.—Psalms 91:11

CHAPTER 5

The Power of Angels

Using Prayer

As we awaken to our loving power within and our true godliness, many of us are now realizing that it is time to lift ourselves away from the trap of physicality and materialism. We find ourselves reaching as never before in our evolutionary pattern toward our highest reconnection with ourselves and with each other. That is why there is such a growing interest in *transcendence*. This age, which is more than 50,000 years in the making, according to the Hindu prophets, is a time for us to evolve into our true selves. As the great spiritual master Jesus of Nazareth said, "All these things I do, you shall do also."

Individuals are questioning whether their needs are of any importance in the grand view of things, and whether their prayers are being heard. You should know that when prayers don't seem to be answered it is not because they aren't being heard. It is because the response is in keeping with the cosmic calendar, unlike our time frame on Earth, and in tune with our soul's most beneficial requirements.

Whether we choose to believe it or not, our prayers are heard and considered. Prayers with prayer beads such as the Catholic rosary or Vedantic Japa Mala are intrinsically powerful because the vibratory level has been built up by thousands of devoted people faithfully repeating the same combination of words for hundreds of years. They raise one's own vibrations, as well as those of the planet. Fervent, faithful, honest prayer is answered the most readily. Prayer by "rote" or repetition, garners a weaker response, but is not without value. Insincere requests, motivated by greed or selfishness do not belong in prayer. The most effective prayers for having our needs met are offered in our own words, expressing simply what is in our hearts and minds.

> In truth, our life is such that its unconscious components are continuously present in all their multiple forms.—Gregory Bateson, *Steps to an Ecology of Mind*

Years ago, when I was teaching yoga on Long Island, and making my way as a psychic counselor—an unheard-of vocation at the time—I was also breaking into regional media. My angels told me the time was right to reach a larger group of people than the local audiences I was used to, and they directed me to broaden my horizons. Television producers, who were beginning to take notice, seemed to agree. But rather than guest appearances or shows as I was promised, I was misused, I felt, by private requests for personal readings, gratis, with hints of something to come. Often I would return messages left by a show's producers, usually long-distance, merely to be met with personal questions about love lives and careers. Now I am not one to object to offering help when one needs it, but these calls made me feel used, and were highly trivial, like "My best friend Elvira is in love with this guy, Johnny, but I know he really loves me—how do I get him to notice me?"

If I tried to steer the conversation to business, the answers were generally evasive, and non-responsive:

"Well, there are other psychics we're considering . . . "

"Well, we haven't made a decision . . . "

Fruitless interviews in offices, during which I was asked for personal readings to higher-ups of higher-ups, gave way to frustration and desire for a career which didn't invite so much self-interest or potential for being used. On my way home one day, I stopped at a church.

"Please," I implored, "let this come to an end. If I am meant to be on television then let it be. If I am not, then let that be."

When I arrived home a message was waiting. It was from a different producer on another show, and a week later I was on Midday Live with Bill Boggs making my national debut.

Spiritual teacher and philosopher Rudolph Steiner conceived of a complex society of angels and spirits as the result of visionary experiences. Angels, according to his system, exist on the first level of consciousness above humankind; above them, in ascending order of levels, are Archangels, Archai (Primal Beginnings), Exusiai (Authorities or Powers), Dynamis (Mights), Kyriotetes (Dominions), Thrones, Cherubim, and Seraphim. Beyond the Seraphim is the Godhead. Each level of being has higher and broader responsibilities in terms of spiritual evolution, beginning with archangels, some of whom are responsible for leading races or nations

While prayer is asking, meditation is waiting, listening, and turning within. As a tool for growth, it enables us to tune into or achieve a higher state of consciousness and awaken awareness of our true selves.

While it may take years of practice and dedication to attain the perfect state of inner peace and universal awareness achieved by master teachers and yogis, sometimes just stopping and turning within can provide you with the answers or the centering you need. Many times when I am looking for something that I simply can't find, or need an answer to a problem, I stop what I'm doing, clear my mind of thoughts, and ask for help. The answer or course of action doesn't come like a thunderbolt, but generally enters my consciousness shortly thereafter.

Prayer is the contemplation of the facts of life from the highest point of view.—Ralph Waldo Emerson, *Self-Reliance*

We have more control over ourselves and our experiences than we acknowledge. We don't live in a haphazard universe where things work out in a hit–or–miss way. There is definite and perfect order to all things. The madness that we frequently see around us is the result of man's improper use of free will.

Humankind's free will, being supreme, is ever being exercised, and is manifest in all phases of life. The Creator, known also as the "The Ancient of Days," or by any variety of names, interacts in and around our free will, in keeping with each person's individual karmic pattern. Angels, ascended masters, saints, guides, and the omniscient "Lords of Karma," who control how karma and prayers interact, are extensions of the Creator. While attuned to our earthly needs, they are bound by the universal laws of karma.

On Not Repeating Mistakes

Author Mark Prophet reports in his book, *The Answer You're Looking for Is Inside of You*, "Saint Germain once told us, 'I made over two million right decisions before I made my ascension.'"

When a karmic lesson is on the soul's agenda, the angels are prevented from intervening. At that point they must pull their protection away from us. Yet if we are open to less-than-severe lessons, the angels will modify our karmic experiences, particularly if we ask for divine protection.

Being aware of our negative tendencies and earnestly trying to correct them can also help prevent karmic "backlash." If we have prayed for protection while driving yet are due to have an accident, instead of a major calamity we may come out with just a minor dent. We may be spared serious damage to life and property if we have learned whatever lessons might have been forthcoming in a more serious accident. Perhaps by changing the habit of leaving home late, which caused you to make up time on the road in a reckless manner, you may have averted more serious repercussions.

> Angels and humankind are but two branches in the family of God, who need to work more closely for the spiritual benefit of humans.—Geoffrey Hodson, *The Brotherhood of Angels and Men*

Turning Within

One night many years ago, I awoke from a terrifying nightmare. I dreamt that my face was being attacked by rats and that I was bleeding to death. Believing then as I do now, in the prophetic character of dreams, I felt keenly that I was at a crossroads, and that my life was nearing its end. I prayed to God, to the angels, and to my guides that this would not happen.

The next day, my brother, sister-in-law, and my husband, Jack, were walking at a beach at the east end of Long Island, New York. As I accidentally walked too close to an old beach wall, my face was suddenly slashed open by a long arm of rusty metal, which was projecting outward. The jagged piece was impossible to see, since it was razor-thin, and I was blinded by the setting sun.

"Don't worry," came the comforting words, "it will be all right." Nearly an hour later, hurtling through Suffolk County to reach a hospital, and having bled through two beach blankets, I was calm, for I had been assured by the voice of God.

God, and all his extensions, are happy to guide, serve, protect, and answer the prayers of humans, not only because we need their assistance, but because they grow in spirit when they work with us. When we work, they work as well—through us, for us, and with us.

> We have more control over ourselves and our experiences than we acknowledge. We don't live in a haphazard universe where things work out in a hit-or-miss way. There is definite and perfect order to all things. The madness that we frequently see around us is the result of man's improper use of free will.
>
> Man's free will, being supreme, is ever being exercised, and is manifest in all phases of life. The Creator, known also as the "The Ancient of Days," "Sunat Kumara," or by any variety of names, interacts in and around man's free will, in keeping with each person's individual karmic pattern. Angels, ascended masters, saints, guides, and the omniscient "Lords of Karma" who control how karma and prayers interact, are extensions of the Creator. While attuned to our earthly needs, they are bound by the universal laws of karma. All human ills arise from some transgression of universal law. The scriptures point out that man must satisfy the laws of nature, while not discrediting the divine omnipotence. He should say: "Lord I trust in Thee, and know Thou canst help me, but I too will do my best to undo any wrong I have done." By a number of means—by prayer, by willpower, by yoga meditation, by consultation with the saints—the adverse effects of past wrongs can be minimized or nullified. Just as a house may be fitted with a copper rod to absorb the shock of lightning, so the bodily temple can be benefited in certain ways.—Master teacher Sri Yukteswar as recounted by Paramahansa Yogananda in *Autobiography of a Yogi* [chapter 16]

Part II

The Karmic Keys

*Discipline does not mean suppression and control,
nor is it adjustment to a pattern or an ideology;
it means a mind that sees "what is,"
and learns from "what is."*

Jiddu Krishnamurti, *The Impossible Question*

CHAPTER 6: KEY 1

Where Is Your Personality (Sun Sign) Taking You?

As most everyone who is familiar with astrology knows, the sun sign indicates the personality. It provides, as Linda Goodman explains in her book, *Sun Signs,* "an amazingly accurate picture of the individual."

We are born as a certain personality and under a certain sign in order to more fully come to a certain type of experience. Being born into Libra, for example, will give one an added sense of beauty and equilibrium. This is especially helpful if the individual has come from a lifetime where he was so imbalanced or perhaps hurt, that he failed to appreciate the beauty around him, and now needs to experience things in a more aesthetic way.

The sun sign, also known as the birth sign, only presents part of the picture. A complete astrological blueprint, known as the natal chart, contains a wheel of twelve houses. Each of these houses indicates a different aspect of the individual. For the purposes of karma, we are primarily concerned with two of these, which make up the next two keys.

The first is the South Node, located in the opposite sign of the North Node. This is where you've "come from," or the Soul Memory. The South Node points to your past-life experience. Usually we have a feeling of saturation or overload in the South Node area. We are just not interested.

The second planetary placement we are concerned with is the North Node. This is why you're here, or the Soul Potential. The North Node indicates the purpose of your birth. It's your karmic responsibility and karmic thrust, or what you're supposed to be doing to get rid of your karmic "indebtedness."

Since the nodes are always in opposite signs, if your South Node is in Gemini, your North Node is in Sagittarius. In this lifetime, this means you are supposed to use the more positive influences of your Gemini energy, such as organization, good listening skills, and a healthy curiosity, to master the opposite energy of your Sagittarian North Node. The problems associated with the South Node must be overcome in order to fully realize the promise of the North Node.

Found in this chapter and the one following are your North and South Node placements, determined by the time of your birth. Learning what these are translates into your steps to overcoming life's problems and achieving your heart's desire.

Look to your birth sign for an indication of your basic personality and the challenges it presents.

Negative traits are the expression of your sun sign's most destructive tendencies. Positive traits are the expression of the most constructive tendencies particular to your sign. While sun signs are only a partial indicator or personality, they are good indicators of the opportunities thrown our way. Negative traits are our opportunity to be challenged in order to grow into the most positive expression of our sign.

ARIES—March 21 to April 20
Negative traits: blunt, arrogant, judgmental, restricted.
Positive traits: courteous, enthusiastic, energetic, loyal.
Most descriptive phrase: "I'm ready! Let's go!"
Happiest Moment: When you're in a position of leadership.
FOR POSITIVE EXPRESSION: Remember to share

TAURUS—April 21 to May 20
Negative traits: self-indulgent, materialistic, inflexible, repressed.
Positive traits: social, careful, vigorous, steadfast.
Most descriptive phrase: "I'm not extravagant, I just like to spend money!"
Happiest Moment: When you get your way.
FOR POSITIVE EXPRESSION: Avoid greed.

GEMINI—May 21 to June 21
Negative traits: unrealistic, compulsive, obsessive, impulsive.
Positive traits: honorable, humorous, adaptable, capable.
Most descriptive phrase: "Who needs to sleep, when there's so much to live and learn?"
Happiest Moment: When you are laughing, talking, and reading all at the same time.
FOR POSITIVE EXPRESSION: Learn to concentrate.

CANCER—June 22 to July 21
Negative traits: rigid, fearful, isolated, passive.
Positive traits: fun-loving, responsible, perceptive, empathic.
Most descriptive phrase: "Why go out to eat, when I can fix us a nice meal?"
Happiest Moment: When you're receiving reciprocal love.
FOR POSITIVE EXPRESSION: Don't be spineless.

LEO—July 22 to August 21
Negative traits: sexually-obsessive, judgmental, opinionated, restricted.
Positive traits: loyal, observant, generous, powerful.
Most descriptive phrase: "Why buy second best?"
Happiest Moment: When you are elected president of anything.
FOR POSITIVE EXPRESSION: Remember humility.

VIRGO—August 22 to September 22
Negative traits: inflexible, puritanical, insistent, procrastinating.
Positive traits: patient, multi-talented, dynamic, free-spirited.
Most descriptive phrase: "Why buy new shoes, when these are perfectly good?"
Happiest Moment: When you find a bargain.
FOR POSITIVE EXPRESSION: Be patient.

LIBRA—September 23 to October 22
Negative traits: insensitive, unforgiving, self-righteous, complacent.
Positive traits: tasteful, socially superior, romantic, capable.

Most descriptive phrase: "I can't decide . . . "
Happiest Moment: While enjoying music and art.
FOR POSITIVE EXPRESSION: Overcome ambivalence.

SCORPIO—October 23 to November 21

Negative traits: procrastinating, depressive, self-unaware, troubled.
Positive traits: influential, powerful, persistent, mystical.
Most descriptive phrase: "I would die before divulging a secret!"
Happiest Moment: While enjoying sensual pleasures.
FOR POSITIVE EXPRESSION: Balance mysticism with the practical world.

SAGITTARIUS—November 22 to December 21

Negative traits: insensitive, domineering, irritating, inscrutable.
Positive traits: daring, indomitable, spiritual, influential.
Most descriptive phrase: "I love life! I love freedom! I love to eat!"
Happiest Moment: While experiencing the majesty of the great outdoors.
FOR POSITIVE EXPRESSION: Extravagance doesn't equal happiness.

CAPRICORN—December 22 to January 19

Negative traits: overconfident, undiplomatic, opinionated, inflexible.
Positive traits: responsible, organized, devoted, structured.
Most descriptive phrase: "What makes you think I need a vacation?"
Happiest Moment: When receiving your paychecks or bankrolls.
FOR POSITIVE EXPRESSION: Learn to lighten up, and enjoy life.

AQUARIUS—January 20 to February 18

Negative traits: self-defeating, immature, impatient, unreliable.
Positive traits: perfectionist, humanitarian, spontaneous, productive.
Most descriptive phrase: "I love everyone. Everyone loves me!"

Happiest Moment: While experiencing cosmic bliss in meditation.
FOR POSITIVE EXPRESSION: Keep your feet on the ground, while looking up.

PISCES—February 19 to March 21
Negative traits: self–indulgent, fearful, withdrawn, overstressed.
Positive traits: intuitive, sensitive, compassionate, youthful.
Most descriptive phrase: "I'm not moody. I just feel things deeply!"
Happiest Moment: When you're rescuing or healing someone.
FOR POSITIVE EXPRESSION: Be compassionate, but not a sponge.

CHAPTER 7: KEY 2

Where Have You Come From?

Your most recent past lifetime is indicated in your birth chart in the position known as the South Node.

The South and North Nodes are not planets. They are referred to as "Nodes of the Moon," and are the points in space where the moon, in its path around the earth, passes through the plane of the earth's orbit around the sun. (See Appendix for Illus.) If the moon is going from the southern hemisphere of the earth to the north, it is called the "North Node." When the moon is going from the northern hemisphere to the south, it is called the "South Node." These Nodes gradually shift through the astrological signs, changing signs about every year-and-a-half. (See Appendix for complete Nodes Chart)

The South Node represents the past-life experiences and relationships which are brought forth to our current lifetime. These include the skills and talents that we have developed as well as our tendencies and habits. The South Node also represents your greatest comfort zones, love and sexual compatibility, as well as areas of difficulties. South Node behaviors feel safe and secure, but offer no new energy toward our soul's growth. Too much concentration in past-life South Node energy can make you feel tired or trapped in a routine. The path is the one of least resistance, and while it feels familiar, it can lead us to a point where we feel hopelessly stuck and unable to change, forever cutting us off from our highest aspirations and any hope of achieving deep and meaningful relationships.

Dwelling too long in South Node energy can create breakdowns in relationships, boredom, lack of challenge, and lead you into a hopeless dead end. It is important to recognize this when it's happening and say to yourself, "been there, done that!" then move on.

But where do you go? How do you shake the patterns that have dogged you for a lifetime, despite psychotherapy, deep introspection, and all your best efforts to change? This is where the North Node comes in. While the South Node represents where you have come from, indicating the habits and tendencies that may be holding you back, the North Node helps to identify what you need to incorporate into your life in order to set your soul free.

I call the South and North Node characteristics, respectively, "Soul Memory," and "Soul Potential."

**Check your birth year to find your Soul Memory.
This is your past-life experience, and indicates
the path which has brought you to the present.**

Soul Memory—GEMINI

Jan. 1, 1900–Dec. 28, 1900
January 20, 1918–August 9, 1919
September 2, 1936–March 21, 1938
April 13, 1955–November 4, 1956
Nov. 23, 1973–June 12, 1975
July 5, 1992–January 21, 1994

In your past life, you were probably involved with public speaking, teaching or writing. On the positive side, you were delightful to be with, because of your multi-faceted, out-going, congenial nature. Your karmic lessons in this lifetime may involve honesty and integrity. In love relationships, you were not always faithful and may have lacked a feeling of loyalty.

INCOMING LIFE LESSON: Be honest and faithful.
PRIMARY CHARACTER WEAKNESS: Impatience, intolerance, and exaggeration of truth.
GENERAL ATTITUDE: "There aren't enough hours in the day to do everything I want to do, and to see everyone I want to see. I need more entertainment, and want to laugh more."
DOMESTIC ATTITUDE: "I almost forgot to have children." "Can

someone please clean my house?"

IN ROMANCE: "Please, take a number."

CAREER: "Let's see, I have four degrees and I can't decide if I should go into TV or publishing. Maybe I should teach English . . . "

FINANCES: "I can put money in the bank tomorrow. I hope I remember."

MOTTO: "Live, laugh, and have fun!"

POSITIVE STRENGTHS: Intelligence, versatility, humor. Life of the party.

GREATEST SOUL CHALLENGE: Learning to concentrate, and to finish jobs that are started. Learning not to laugh at the wrong time.

DAILY ASSERTION: I will not gloss over everything and will take time to stop and smell the roses.

Soul Memory—TAURUS

Dec. 29, 1901–July 17, 1902
August 10, 1919–February 26, 1921
March 22, 1938–October 9, 1939
Nov. 5, 1956–May 21, 1958
June 13, 1975–December 29, 1976
January 22, 1994–August 11, 1995

In your past life, you were probably involved with merchandising, trading, or banking. Friends and loved ones could always count on you, because of your stable nature. Your karmic lessons may be involved with learning how to be more adaptable and flexible. You also stubbornly stuck by your own beliefs, ignoring whether they hurt or helped others.

INCOMING LIFE–LESSON: Be flexible, stay sensitive.

PRIMARY CHARACTER WEAKNESS: Materialism and greed.

GENERAL ATTITUDE: "Acquiring wealth is all that matters."

IN ROMANCE: "I'm faithful, but I can't get enough sex."

CAREER: "Get out of my way. I'm moving up!" Goal–oriented, power–driven.

FINANCES: "I love to have, count, and spend money!"
MOTTO: "I want it all!"
POSITIVE STRENGTHS: Stability, perseverance.
GREATEST SOUL CHALLENGE: To learn about flexibility of thought and action. To respect hedonism, but not to give in to it.

DAILY ASSERTION: Sharing what I have with others will make me happier than I am now.

Soul Memory—ARIES
July 18, 1902–February 4, 1904
February 27, 1921–September 15, 1922
October 10, 1939–April 27, 1941
November 29, 1928–June 18, 1930
May 22, 1958–December 8, 1959
August 12, 1995–February 27, 1997

In your past life, you were probably involved with finance, taxation, hunting, or the militia. You did not always feel or express sensitivity to others, and often attributed it to your job's responsibilities. You traveled frequently, and appreciated the opportunity of being distanced from your loved ones and domestic responsibilities. You were always courageous, but not always sensitive to the needs of others.
INCOMING LIFE LESSON: Express sensitivity to the needs of others.
PRIMARY CHARACTER WEAKNESS: Ego and a lust for power that often overrides conscience.
GENERAL ATTITUDE: "My compulsive pursuit of my own plans, ideas, or agendas is commendable, even if other people might be hurt or distressed."
DOMESTIC RELATIONSHIPS: A tendency toward abusive, arrogant, and combative confrontational attitude toward family members.
IN ROMANCE: "Do it my way, Baby!" A tendency towards a domineering, bored, impatient attitude.
CAREER: "I deserve a raise!" Quick-tempered, along with reckless

career moves may characterize your attempt at the upward climb. **FINANCES:** "I expect to have it all!" Characterized by carefree spending, often lacking realistic awareness of financial situation. **PAST–LIFE MOTTO TO BREAK:** "Me, first. After that, me!" **POSITIVE STRENGTHS:** A natural leader, who always exudes self–confidence. An exciting, enthusiastic attitude. A dependable, loving relative; reliable friend; passionate; and a tireless lover. Generous to a fault. **GREATEST SOUL CHALLENGE:** Development of consideration for others.

DAILY ASSERTION: I am filled with God-empowerment. I do not have to prove anything to anyone. I am happy, safe, and secure.

Soul Memory—PISCES
February 5, 1904–August 23, 1905
September 16, 1922–April 4, 1924
April 28, 1941–November 15, 1942
December 9, 1959–July 3, 1961
July 20, 1978–February 5, 1980
February 28, 1997–September 17, 1998

In your past life, you may have put your love of mysticism and metaphysics above the needs of your family and loved ones, including those who were dependent upon you. You may also have been so enmeshed in your love of healing and medicine that you ignored the needs of your own body, along with the well–being of those who depended upon you.

INCOMING LIFE–LESSON: Be aware. Acknowledge and deal with the needs of your family, and your own body.

PRIMARY CHARACTER WEAKNESS: Self–destructive tendencies, moodiness, and over–sensitivity.

GENERAL ATTITUDE: "Of course it's my fault."

DOMESTIC ATTITUDE: "Those who are hurting or needy feel like they are my children. I will help them and I will help my real children. I can heal your pain."

IN ROMANCE: "Do you think I have beautiful feet? Let me see yours! Can you walk on my back?"

CAREER: "Let's see, should I be a podiatrist, chiropractor, nurse, or chef?"

FINANCES: "I spent all of my money on shoes and food. I forgot to go to the bank to make a deposit."

MOTTO: "A dose of reality goes a long way. Also, no more guilt! Not everything that goes wrong is my fault."

POSITIVE STRENGTHS: Tender, caring heart, and compassionate nature.

GREATEST SOUL CHALLENGE: Learning to survive in a tough world. Not giving in to mind-altering substances or addictions of any kind to deal with any kind of pain.

DAILY ASSERTION: Not everything that goes wrong is my fault. It just seems that way.

Soul Memory—AQUARIUS

August 24, 1905–March 13, 1907
April 5, 1924–October 22, 1925
November 16, 1942–June 3, 1944
July 4, 1961–January 13, 1963
February 6, 1980–August 25, 1981
September 18, 1998–April 5, 2000

In your past life, you may have been so involved in what you considered important humanitarian pursuits, that you neglected your very own family. Charitable pursuits always captured your attention, above everything else. In addition, your love for exploring and adventure, and desire to "find yourself," left lonely neglected loved ones.

INCOMING LIFE LESSON: Charity begins at home.

PRIMARY CHARACTER WEAKNESS: Spreading one's self too thin.

GENERAL ATTITUDE: "I will save the world!"

DOMESTIC ATTITUDE: "Helping strangers may be more important than addressing the needs of my family. Oh, don't worry. My family is well taken care of!"

IN ROMANCE: "How can I love just one person, when I belong to the universe?"

CAREER: "Let's see, should I be a firefighter, police officer, or social worker?"

FINANCES: "Why should I put money in a bank, when I can give it to homeless people?"

MOTTO: "Life is so rewarding when strangers need and love you."

POSITIVE STRENGTHS: Humanitarianism, with a sincere desire to serve others.

GREATEST SOUL CHALLENGE: Getting your priorities in order. Recognizing where your presence is required.

DAILY ASSERTION: Charity begins at home.

Soul Memory—CAPRICORN
March 14, 1907–September 29, 1908
October 23, 1925–May 12, 1927
June 4, 1944–December 23, 1945
January 14, 1963–August 5, 1964
August 26, 1981–March 14, 1983
April 6, 2000–October 12, 2001

In your past life, you excelled at all forms of selling, teaching, and business. While basically honest, in your desire to accomplish goals and financial success, you may well have overlooked your spiritual growth and needs of mates and children. Always focused and concentrated, you may have missed the big picture, one that involved the expression of human compassion.

INCOMING LIFE-LESSON: Be loving and compassionate. Put people ahead of money.

PRIMARY CHARACTER WEAKNESS: Tendency to concentrate too much and being a workaholic.

GENERAL ATTITUDE: "There aren't enough hours in the day to do all of my work. You have more work for me? No problem."

DOMESTIC ATTITUDE: "If I teach my children at home, they will have a better education. No one is a better teacher than I am."

IN ROMANCE: "We can make love after I paint the house, shop for groceries, cement the walk, repair the fence, call my mother, feed the dog . . . "

CAREER: "I will be the head of the corporation, because it is my company."

FINANCES: "I am not a miser! I am just a practical person who respects money, and likes to save it, keep it, and have it. No, I don't have to share it."

MOTTO: "An honest day's work, for an honest day's dollar. I will not get carried away with my own importance, or feelings of having to deal with burdensome responsibilities."

POSITIVE STRENGTHS: Ability to finish a job; practical, sensible, attitudes and values. Extraordinary teaching and executive abilities.

GREATEST SOUL CHALLENGE: Learning that you do not have to do everything yourself, and that you should trust others to assist you in your endeavors.

DAILY ASSERTION: No man (or woman) is an island.

Soul Memory—SAGITTARIUS
September 30, 1908–April 18, 1910
May 13, 1927–November 28, 1928
December 24, 1945–July 11, 1947
August 6, 1964–February 21, 1966
March 15, 1983–October 1, 1984

In your past life, you made a great deal of money, and spent a great deal of money. You may well have been involved in gambling, banking, travel or sports. Always courageous, you went where others feared to tread. You were always an adventurer, and loved danger and excitement. You were always up for a challenge and a thrill, even if it caused your loved ones great distress and heartbreak.

INCOMING LIFE LESSON: Be aware of the fact that your actions can cause great pain or distress to others.

PRIMARY CHARACTER WEAKNESS: Overindulgence in food and laziness. Tendency to be stubborn or inflexible.

GENERAL ATTITUDE: "I'm hungry, so I'll eat it."

DOMESTIC ATTITUDE: "Let's get the biggest house on the block, with the biggest kitchen, and the biggest yard, with a big garage for our big cars!"

IN ROMANCE: "Let's make love outdoors, or in a moving vehicle!"

CAREER: "I hope it involves travel!"

FINANCES: "Sure, I have a huge amount of money. I love to make it, and I love to touch it, smell it, see it, and spend it! Want some? Let's go out to dinner. I'll treat!"

MOTTO: "Life is fun!"

POSITIVE STRENGTHS: Generosity and a good sense of humor.

GREATEST SOUL CHALLENGE: Learning to see the broad picture, without wearing blinders.

DAILY ASSERTION: I recognize the importance of increasing my peripheral vision, and seeing the big picture.

Soul Memory—SCORPIO

April 19, 1910–November 7, 1911
November 29, 1928–June 18, 1930
July 12, 1947–January 28, 1949
February 22, 1966–September 9, 1967
October 2, 1984–April 20, 1986

In your past life you were easily bored, especially with domestic situations. This may well have put you in compromising positions, and may have involved you in the dark underbelly of society. However, you also had a mystical side, and often soared to the highest of spiritual heights. In desperation, however, there may also have been those times of dwelling in the lowest and most dangerous of realms.

INCOMING LIFE LESSON: Learn discernment, raise your sights toward our Creator, or the Universal Truth.

PRIMARY CHARACTER WEAKNESS: Too much passion that rules most decisions.

GENERAL ATTITUDE: "I have a secret, and you'll never know what it is."

DOMESTIC ATTITUDE: "Where can I hide my porn so that no one can find it?"

IN ROMANCE: "Sex is good. Sex keeps you young. Sex keeps you healthy!"

CAREER: "I'd make a great detective, but I also love being a mystic!"

FINANCES: "Where can I hide my money?"

MOTTO: "There's nothing more important than sex, mysticism, and secrets!"

POSITIVE STRENGTHS: Great investigative nature, can be trusted with secrets, can unravel mysteries.

GREATEST SOUL CHALLENGE: Learning to trust others. Staying virtuous.

DAILY ASSERTION: My life is an honest, open book.

Soul Memory—LIBRA

November 8, 1911–May 26, 1913
June 19, 1930–January 6, 1932
January 29, 1949–August 17, 1950
September 10, 1967–March 28, 1969
April 21, 1986–November 8, 1987

In your past life you may have enmeshed yourself in a world of artistic or musical creativity. Often neglecting the needs of your own body, you often failed to meet financial and domestic responsibilities, in the name of "art." You may have neglected loved ones and your own health, in your desire to create artistic or musical perfection.

INCOMING LIFE–LESSON: Don't lose a grip on the realities of life, and your responsibilities.

PRIMARY CHARACTER WEAKNESS: Ambivalence and lack of reality.

GENERAL ATTITUDE: "Either one is good. I can't decide. The good news, however, is that I look good, while trying to decide."

DOMESTIC ATTITUDE: "Should we stay in or go out? Should I call someone or do this myself? I can't decide!"

IN ROMANCE: "I love them both!"

CAREER: "Should I be a lawyer or interior decorator? I can't decide."

FINANCES: "Is there something wrong with spending my entire salary on looking good?"

MOTTO: "Maybe I'll take one of each."

POSITIVE STRENGTHS: Ability to see both sides of an issue, and to bring harmony and balance to all involvements.

GREATEST SOUL CHALLENGE: To learn to make a decision and stand by it.

DAILY ASSERTION: I know what I want! I know what I want! I know what I want!

Soul Memory—VIRGO

May 27, 1913–December 13, 1914
January 7, 1932–July 25, 1933
August 18, 1950–March 7, 1952
March 29, 1969–October 15, 1970
November 9, 1987–May 28, 1989

In your past life you were probably involved in the medical field. You may have abandoned everything and everyone close to you, for the admirable calling from the battlefield or from those who were ill and dying. Perhaps your great concentration to help those who were in great need, caused you to neglect growth in other areas, or to learn how to enjoy life.

INCOMING LIFE LESSON: Don't hide behind responsibilities; rather, face your own emotions, needs, and pleasures.

PRIMARY CHARACTER WEAKNESS: Tendency to be too modest and detail–oriented. Failure to see the big picture.

GENERAL ATTITUDE: "Don't worry. Leave it to me. I can do it while you rest. Even if I get grumpy, I'll do it right, but it may take a little bit longer than you had planned. Trust me, it will be worth it."

DOMESTIC ATTITUDE: "Is that a crumb on the counter?"

IN ROMANCE: "Let's change the sheets again, and take another shower. I'll brush my teeth again, while you trim your nails."

CAREER: "Why should I care about money? All that matters is that I do my job well, and serve others with kindness and consideration. Work all weekend? No problem."

FINANCES: "Why spend good money, when we can do it ourselves?

MOTTO: "Being practical and clean is next to godliness."

POSITIVE STRENGTHS: Reliability, independence.

GREATEST SOUL CHALLENGE: Learning to lighten up, and not get caught in meaningless pursuits or details.

DAILY ASSERTION: I will look at the big picture and not get caught up in details.

Soul Memory—LEO

December 14, 1914–July 2, 1916
July 26, 1933–February 12, 1935
March 8, 1952–October 2, 1953
October 16, 1970–May 5, 1972
May 29, 1989–December 15, 1990

In your past life, you were probably used to performing in the public eye. You were used to applause or acclaim, and may even have been part of a royal blood line. Your nature may have become quite self-centered, with an overly inflated ego. Compromise may not have always been your calling card, and you may have lacked sensitivity for the feelings and needs of others.

INCOMING LIFE LESSON: Remember what happened to Marie Antoinette, when, with regard to starving peasants, she said, "Let them eat cake!"

PRIMARY CHARACTER WEAKNESS: Ego, drive for control and power. Ignoring the pain of others.

GENERAL ATTITUDE: "I'm here now! Everything can begin!"

DOMESTIC ATTITUDE: "No child of mine can look poor, or have less than other people. My car, clothing, and home have to be the best. We must have the best of everything. Why? Because I deserve it, that's why."

IN ROMANCE: "You're a nice guy, but are you ever going to be the head of your company? When we're in bed, can I be on top?"

CAREER: "How long before I get the head office with the desk overlooking the city?"

FINANCES: "No one deserves wealth and power more than I do!"
MOTTO: "It's mine! And, it's the best!"
POSITIVE STRENGTHS: Honesty, integrity, reliability.
GREATEST SOUL CHALLENGE: Learning humility.

DAILY ASSERTION: Sure, I'm terrific, but so are a lot of other people.

Soul Memory—CANCER
July 3, 1916–January 19, 1918
February 13, 1935–September 1, 1926
October 3, 1953–April 12, 1955
May 6, 1972–November 22, 1973
December 16, 1990–July 4, 1992

In your past life, employed as chef, caretaker, teacher, or parent, you may have been too involved in nurturing others, and yourself. This is particularly with regard to food and drink. You may have frequently overindulged to the great detriment of your physical body. In addition, you did not always respect and properly care for your health, and felt that it was within your rights to enjoy whatever brought you the greatest satisfaction and pleasure.
INCOMING LIFE LESSON: Keep your priorities in order. Don't neglect your body, mind or spirit.
PRIMARY CHARACTER WEAKNESS: Withdrawal into a shell, instead of dealing head-on with issues or problems.
GENERAL ATTITUDE: "I'm vulnerable, sensitive, and sweet. Don't hurt my feelings." Clingy nature.
DOMESTIC ATTITUDE: "How can I keep my children from leaving home, ever?"
IN ROMANCE: "Let me take care of you. Let me feed you. I will keep you warm, safe, and cozy, but please cover me when I'm cold."
CAREER: Ideal careers involve nurturing those in need, or feeding those who are hungry. Amazing, patient, teaching abilities.
FINANCES: "How can I feel secure, if we don't have a lot of money in the bank and a big, cozy, comfortable house, with very comfortable furniture?"

MOTTO: "There's nothing more important than mothering and feeding each other."

POSITIVE STRENGTHS: Compassion, ability to express love and tenderness.

GREATEST SOUL CHALLENGE: Staying emotionally strong, and not retreating into a shell when frightened. Working to avoid feelings of mental or emotional vulnerability.

DAILY ASSERTION: I can do it!

CHAPTER 8: KEY 3

What Is Your Potential?

Find your birth year to discern your Soul Potential, current life lessons, health, money and success issues, and your soul mates.

Soul Potential—SAGITTARIUS

Jan. 1, 1900–Dec. 28, 1900
January 20, 1918–August 9, 1919
September 2, 1936–March 21, 1938
April 13, 1955–November 4, 1956
Nov. 23, 1973–June 12, 1975
July 5, 1992–January 21, 1994

LESSON FOR REACHING POTENTIAL: Your love for freedom and excitement should not cause distress to others. Everything in moderation.

HEALTH: Avoid excesses, including exercise and food.

GENERAL ATTITUDE: "I can have it all. All I have to do is be very honest and work hard."

DOMESTIC RELATIONSHIPS: "Children are great, even if we have to spend a fortune to feed them and send them to the best schools. Nothing is too good for my family."

ROMANTIC RELATIONSHIPS: "I will always be true–blue, faithful, and honest."

SOUL MATE: Best soul mate is born under the sign of Gemini, Libra, or Aquarius.

HOW TO SUCCESSFULLY LINK UP WITH YOUR SOUL MATE: Go to a party or wedding. Socialize. Entertain and have your friends bring their friends. Laugh, live, enjoy yourself. It will happen.

YOUR MOST SUCCESSFUL CAREER PATH: Many North Node Sagittarians are involved in the medical or business field, which is really quite perfect. You are also excellent managers of corporations. You will be prosperous, and never at a loss for activity.

YOUR GREATEST KEY TO LASTING WEALTH AND PROSPERITY: You are usually much focused, which is the primary key to your lasting wealth and prosperity. No need to scatter your energies. Stay on track, and let the prosperity and wealth happen. It will!

GREATEST KEY TO SUCCESSFUL AND PERMANENT WEIGHT LOSS: Use this affirmation three times a day for the rest of your life. Let it flow deeply into your consciousness: "Less of me, Dear Lord, and more of you, will permanently bring about the weight loss that will help me to be healthy, strong, and attractive. Thank you for your support and guidance."

GREATEST LIFE CHALLENGE: Learning to diversify, or become more versatile, if the occasion calls for it. Learn to economize.

DAILY MEDITATION AND AFFIRMATION FOR YOUR GREATEST SOUL GROWTH AND PSYCHIC DEVELOPMENT: "Money is not the most important thing in the universe. I will listen to, and respect, the message from my soul. I will meditate and read. I will also take off my blinders if I am wearing them.

Soul Potential—SCORPIO
Dec. 29, 1901–July 17, 1902
August 10, 1919–February 26, 1921
March 22, 1938–October 9, 1939
Nov. 5, 1956–May 21, 1958
June 13, 1975–December 29, 1976
January 22, 1994–August 11, 1995

LESSON FOR REACHING POTENTIAL: When you have a choice about soaring high in God's heaven, or scraping along the ground, soar like an eagle!

HEALTH: Don't neglect the parts of your body that you cannot see.

GENERAL ATTITUDE: "You can tell me anything! My lips are sealed! I love secrets and mysteries." I will always keep secrets to myself! I also want to know about universal secrets. "Oh, and did I tell you how much I love sex?"

DOMESTIC RELATIONSHIPS: "Family life is great, but just make sure we have company as often as possible. Make sure they are attractive and sexy, though."

ROMANTIC RELATIONSHIPS: "It's difficult to just be romantic, since my hormones are always working overtime. Let's move things to the next level, as soon as possible."

SOUL MATE: Your best soul mates are born under the signs of Taurus, Virgo, or Capricorn.

HOW TO SUCCESSFULLY LINK UP WITH YOUR SOUL MATE: Scorpios are among the most metaphysical, psychic, and spiritual of all people when they function at their highest levels. A perfect place for you to meet your soul mate is in a yoga class or at the gym. Walking is a great form of moving meditation, which can often link soul mates together.

MOST SUCCESSFUL CAREER PATH: Mystical careers, such as teaching psychic development or yoga, are perfect for North Node Scorpios, as well as writing careers that deal with the mysteries of life.

GREATEST KEY TO YOUR WEALTH AND PROSPERITY: Doors to your greatest wealth and prosperity open for you when you start listening to what your heart and mind are telling you, which will definitely cause you to march to a different drummer. Do not allow yourself to be pigeon-holed into a conventional career that may not be right for you.

GREATEST KEY TO LASTING AND PERMANENT WEIGHT LOSS: Use this affirmation three times a day for the rest of your life. Let it flow deeply into your consciousness: "Less of me, Dear Lord, and more of you will permanently bring about the weight loss that will help me to be health, strong, and attractive. Thank you for your support and guidance."

GREATEST CHALLENGE: Having the confidence in yourself to follow your own dreams, even if others consider you to be out of step and iconoclastic. Revel in your uniqueness.

DAILY MEDITATION AND AFFIRMATION FOR YOUR GREATEST SOUL GROWTH AND PSYCHIC DEVELOP-

MENT: "To thine own self be true." Do not be swayed by people who feel that they know what's best for you.

Soul Potential—LIBRA

July 18, 1902–February 4, 1904
February 27, 1921–September 15, 1922
October 10, 1939–April 27, 1941
May 22, 1958–December 8, 1959
November 29, 1928–June 18, 1930
August 12, 1995–February 27, 1997

LESSON FOR REACHING POTENTIAL: Don't be so concerned about doing the "right" thing, or about being fair, or about the "proper balance," of things, or it will be too late to do anything! Don't miss the boat.

HEALTH: Take especially good care of your kidneys and blood.

MOST IMPORTANT LIFE LESSON: To overcome ambivalence and the need to please everyone. Main life lesson is most likely that you have to learn to develop a belief system, and to stand up for your beliefs.

GENERAL ATTITUDE SHOULD BE: "Sure, I can see both sides of an issue, but I will learn to decide which side is correct, and act on that decision."

DOMESTIC ATTITUDE MIGHT BE: "It's not right to be a push-over or to be spineless when people are depending upon me."

ROMANTIC ATTITUDE MIGHT BE: "Yes, they're all good-looking, but I will choose just one and stick with that choice!"

SOUL MATE: Aries, Sagittarius, and Leo.

HOW TO SUCCESSFULLY LINK UP WITH YOUR SOUL MATE: Taking into consideration that you are the sign of "the scales," you are naturally drawn to everything related to law, including dating and marrying a lawyer. Therefore, being in the atmosphere of courtrooms, or places where lawyers congregate is highly recommended when seeking your ideal soul mate.

MOST SUCCESSFUL CAREER PATH: Careers that best use your artistic talent, creative flair, or are involved with law or justice.

GREATEST KEY TO YOUR WEALTH AND PROSPERITY: Your

lifelong goal might be to know in your heart, soul, and mind that, while looking great is important, it's also important to save money for that rainy day. Most important of all, do something that you love.

GREATEST KEY TO LASTING AND PERMANENT WEIGHT LOSS: Use this affirmation three times a day for the rest of your life. Let it flow deeply into your consciousness: "Less of me, Dear Lord, and more of you will permanently bring about the weight loss that will help me to be healthy, strong, and attractive. Thank you for your support and guidance."

LIFE GOAL: To learn to make a decision, and to stick to it.

GREATEST CHALLENGE: To stop analyzing everything to death! Think about it, and then do something! Also, don't be blown away by superficial standards and good looks.

DAILY MEDITATION AND AFFIRMATION FOR YOUR GREATEST SOUL GROWTH AND PSYCHIC DEVELOP-MENT: "Since we are on the earth only a short time, I will make the best use of that time by learning to take a stand, and then not backsliding. I will also stop analyzing everything."

Soul Potential—VIRGO

February 5, 1904–August 23, 1905
September 16, 1922–April 4, 1924
April 28, 1941–November 15, 1942
December 9, 1959–July 3, 1961
July 20, 1978–February 5, 1980
February 28, 1997–September 17, 1998

LESSON FOR REACHING POTENTIAL: Don't get caught up with the small stuff; look at the big picture. Life is too short to lose yourself in the details.

HEALTH: Protect your intestinal tract. Eat wisely.

MOST IMPORTANT LIFE LESSON: Understanding that service to others is fine, but that you shouldn't lose yourself.

GENERAL ATTITUDE SHOULD BE: "I will take care of others, and my responsibilities, and I won't get lost in the details. I will try to see the Big Picture."

DOMESTIC ATTITUDE MIGHT BE: "While I appreciate clean–liness, I won't put my need for cleanliness and neatness ahead of the happiness of my family."

ROMANTIC ATTITUDE MIGHT BE: "I won't be a big fud–dy–duddy. I will appreciate this person's finer qualities, while trying to ignore those little annoying shortcomings!"

SOUL MATE: Pisces, Scorpio, and Cancer.

HOW TO SUCCESSFULLY LINK UP WITH YOUR SOUL MATE: Forget the contact lenses. Don't be afraid to wear those eyeglasses. Forget that they called you "four–eyes" in school. Your potential soul mate will be blown away with your mercurial wit and intelligence . . . not to mention your impeccably groomed hair, nails, and outfit. Project that you are a model of class and elegance!

MOST SUCCESSFUL CAREER PATH: Careers involved with finances, service, anything detail–oriented, drama, the stage, radio, creation of television and radio shows and their production.

GREATEST KEY TO YOUR WEALTH AND PROSPERITY: Learn to rise above the small–thinking, self–limiting attitudes of failure for the greatest financial success and remuneration. When you do a job, do not get carried away with the details.

YOUR KEY TO SUCCESSFUL AND PERMANENT WEIGHT LOSS: Use this affirmation three times a day for the rest of your life. Let it flow deeply into your consciousness: "Less of me, Dear Lord, and more of you will permanently bring about the weight loss that will help me to be healthy, strong, and attractive. Thank you for your support and guidance."

GREATEST LIFE GOAL: To learn to fly freely, and to fly high, without self–limiting thought, fears, or actions.

GREATEST CHALLENGE: To "get" the big picture in anything and everything in your life.

DAILY MEDITATION AND AFFIRMATION FOR YOUR GREATEST SOUL GROWTH AND PSYCHIC DEVELOP–MENT: "I have no place in my life for small, restrictive thoughts. I will fly high, and soar with the eagles!"

Soul Potential—LEO

August 24, 1905–March 13, 1907
April 5, 1924–October 22, 1925
November 16, 1942–June 3, 1944
July 4, 1961–January 13, 1963
February 6, 1980–August 25, 1981
September 18, 1998–April 5, 2000

LESSON FOR REACHING POTENTIAL: You aren't the "King of the Hill." No one is indispensable. Get over yourself.
HEALTH: Take care of your circulation and your heart.
MOST IMPORTANT LIFE LESSON: Learning to control your ego and love of power.
GENERAL ATTITUDE SHOULD BE: "Let's put on a play, starring me, of course, but I'll do it without feeling superior to everyone."
DOMESTIC ATTITUDE MIGHT BE: "You are my children and I want the world to see you in the best possible light, but we'll greet everyone with humility, poise, and grace."
ROMANTIC ATTITUDE MIGHT BE: "I am passionate, and will marry for love, not for social position or money."
SOUL MATE: Aquarius, Gemini, or Libra.
HOW TO SUCCESSFULLY LINK UP WITH YOUR SOUL MATE: Show that magnificent leonine mane, for starters. Be bold, courageous, and daring! Shine in a crowd, not only with your appearance, but also with your daring attitude. Use your jungle–radar to scope out the room, boldly walk up to that person, and ask for a date.
MOST SUCCESSFUL CAREER PATH: Any position that allows you to shine, teach, or direct others.
GREATEST KEY TO YOUR WEALTH AND PROSPERITY: You are the essence of honesty and integrity, but will go to great lengths to look wealthy. This is fine if you don't stress and strain, trying to impress everyone.
YOUR KEY TO SUCCESSFUL AND PERMANENT WEIGHT LOSS: Use this affirmation three times a day for the rest of your life, letting it flow deeply into your consciousness: "Less of me, Dear Lord, and more of you, will permanently bring about the weight loss that will help me to be healthy, strong, and attractive.

Thank you for your support and guidance."

LIFE GOAL: To be Number One in just about everything. That's OK, if you do it with humility in your **heart, soul, and mind.**

GREATEST CHALLENGE: Learning to respect and honor the accomplishments of others.

DAILY MEDITATION AND AFFIRMATION FOR YOUR GREATEST SOUL GROWTH AND PSYCHIC DEVELOP-MENT: "OK, I know I'm good. In fact, I'm almost perfect. However, I will not lose my humility and consideration for others."

Soul Potential—CANCER

March 14, 1907–September 29, 1908
October 23, 1925–May 12, 1927
June 4, 1944–December 23, 1945
January 14, 1963–August 5, 1964
August 26, 1981–March 14, 1983
April 6, 2000–October 12, 2001

LESSON FOR REACHING POTENTIAL: You aren't the only sensitive, moody person on the planet. We all have feelings. Stop hiding when your feelings are hurt. Deal with it.

HEALTH: Your stomach will be much better if you avoid stress and meditate.

MOST IMPORTANT LIFE LESSON: Expression of devotion to family, loved ones, without becoming obsessed and excluding the rest of the world.

GENERAL ATTITUDE SHOULD BE: "I love my family, but don't want them to be completely dependent upon me."

DOMESTIC RELATIONSHIPS: Ideal attitude might be: "I look forward to my little birdies growing up, becoming successful, and leaving the nest."

ROMANTIC RELATIONSHIPS: Ideal attitude might be: "I am confident enough to know that you will come back to me." Rise above romantic insecurities.

SOUL MATE: Ideal partner might be Capricorn, Taurus, or Virgo.

HOW TO SUCCESSFULLY LINK UP WITH YOUR SOUL MATE: The key to connecting and linking up with your soul mate is often based on the Cancerian ability to nurture others. In other words, use your lovable, caring nature to communicate your feelings, and back up those feelings with some great home-cooking.

MOST SUCCESSFUL CAREER PATH: Best expression of a Cancerian karmic path would be any career involving nurturing, or the medical field, food preparation, or teaching.

GREATEST KEY TO YOUR WEALTH AND PROSPERITY: Best attitude for soul satisfaction would involve creating a feeling of security, and a nest egg, which comes with the ownership of at least one comfortable, cozy home. Become involved with real estate.

YOUR KEY TO SUCCESSFUL AND PERMANENT WEIGHT LOSS: Use this affirmation three times a day for the rest of your life, letting it flow deeply into your consciousness: "Less of me, Dear Lord, and more of you will permanently bring about the weight loss that will help me to be healthy, strong, and attractive. Thank you for your support and guidance."

GREATEST LIFE GOAL: Teaching others, teaching children, healing, and helping others.

GREATEST CHALLENGE: Don't allow yourself to get lost in the nurturing process.

DAILY MEDITATION AND AFFIRMATION FOR YOUR GREATEST SOUL GROWTH AND PSYCHIC DEVELOPMENT: "I am happy that I have the ability to care for and love those around me, but I will not lose myself in the process."

Soul Potential—GEMINI
September 30, 1908–April 18, 1910
May 13, 1927–November 28, 1928
December 24, 1945–July 11, 1947
August 6, 1964–February 21, 1966
March 15, 1983–October 1, 1984

LESSON FOR REACHING POTENTIAL: Don't scatter your energies. Meditate and study; learn who you are, and what your abilities are. Try to concentrate your efforts.

HEALTH: Don't stress your nervous system. Laugh, and release tension.

MOST IMPORTANT LIFE LESSON: Learning to stay flexible, yet staying on target with realistic goals.

GENERAL ATTITUDE: "I can do it, as long as it's not boring."

DOMESTIC RELATIONSHIPS: Greatest life lesson comes with the test of your patience as a parent, since you are usually impatient and high-strung. "Of course I'll play with you and read to you, my little darlings!" Also, do not snap at your mate. Discuss differences with patience.

ROMANTIC RELATIONSHIPS: Greatest life lessons come with your ability to stay faithful to one person. "Do you think you could please wear different costumes, or outfits, every time I see you, dear? Also, while you are at it, can you please read the newspaper and discuss it with me?"

SOUL MATE: Greatest love compatibility can come with Sagittarius, Aries, and Leo.

HOW TO SUCCESSFULLY LINK UP WITH YOUR SOUL MATE: Go to places that you love—like bookstores, the library, computer stores, and Wi-Fi coffee shops. Your soul mate has to be intelligent, fun, and verbally interactive. Strike up conversations.

MOST SUCCESSFUL CAREER PATH: Any career involving media communication, writing, or speaking. "I can be a radio host? You don't even have to pay me!"

GREATEST KEY TO YOUR WEALTH AND PROSPERITY: Greatest life lessons involve being practical and sensible about money, and not just spending it irresponsibly or because of a love of variety or change. "I guess we should pay that bill and not go out to eat tonight." Learn how to handle your finances yourself. Don't run from financial responsibilities.

YOUR KEY TO SUCCESSFUL AND PERMANENT WEIGHT LOSS: Use this affirmation three times a day, for the rest of your life, letting it flow deeply into your consciousness: "Less of me, Dear Lord, and more of you, will permanently bring about the weight loss that will help me to be healthy, strong, and attractive. Thank you for your support and guidance."

LIFE GOALS: To achieve maximum expression of mental abilities.

GREATEST CHALLENGE: Greatest life lesson involves staying on target and not vacillating when having to make a decision.

DAILY MEDITATION AND AFFIRMATION FOR YOUR GREATEST SOUL GROWTH AND PSYCHIC DEVELOP-MENT: "I may be bored, but I'm going to finish this, even if it's the last thing I do!"

Soul Potential—TAURUS

April 19, 1910–November 7, 1911
November 29, 1928–June 18, 1930
July 12, 1947–January 28, 1949
February 22, 1966–September 9, 1967
October 2, 1984–April 20, 1986

LESSON FOR REACHING POTENTIAL: Loosen up. Life is too short to be so rigid and uncompromising. Don't take money so seriously.

HEALTH: Don't overeat, exercise. This is especially important for you.

MOST IMPORTANT LIFE LESSONS: Lessons that involve your integrity and your ability to rise above the "greed factor."

LIFE GOAL: Security. To acquire wealth without compromising your honesty.

GENERAL ATTITUDE SHOULD BE: "I want to express reliability. You can count on me!"

DOMESTIC ATTITUDE MIGHT BE: Since your greatest life lessons involve achieving family serenity and financial security, but being happy and content in whatever state you are in: "We don't have to be wealthy, but I'm happy as long as we're a family."

ROMANTIC ATTITUDE MIGHT BE: Since expressing fidelity and passion are key karmic factors: "We don't need a lot of sex, unless, of course you also think it's a good idea! Let's be faithful, forever!"

SOUL MATES: Greatest life lessons come with Scorpio, Cancer, and Pisces.

HOW TO SUCCESSFULLY LINK UP WITH YOUR SOUL MATE: Your naturally passionate nature acts as a love magnet, so allow your sensuality to shine! Don't hide that sexy light under a bushel. Develop a body-enhancing wardrobe and walk with pride and sensuality.

MOST SUCCESSFUL CAREER PATH: Greatest life satisfaction and success comes with careers involved with money and managing your own business.

KEY TO CREATING YOUR GREATEST WEALTH AND PROSPERITY: Life lesson involves learning to share without expecting repayment or obligation. Be charitable, generous, and non-judgmental about the material wealth of others.

KEY TO YOUR SUCCESSFUL AND PERMANENT WEIGHT LOSS: Use this affirmation three times a day, for the rest of your life, letting it flow deeply into your consciousness: "Less of me, Dear Lord, and more of you, will permanently bring about the weight loss that will help me to be healthy, strong, and attractive. Thank you for your support and guidance."

LIFE GOAL: To be wealthy and debt-free, but also spiritually enlightened.

GREATEST CHALLENGE: Keeping flexible thought patterns, not being stubborn or rigid, and able to let new ideas and concepts flow into your consciousness.

DAILY MEDITATION AND AFFIRMATION FOR YOUR GREATEST SOUL GROWTH AND PSYCHIC DEVELOPMENT: "Honor is more important than prosperity."

Soul Potential—ARIES
November 8, 1911–May 26, 1913
June 19, 1930–January 6, 1932
January 29, 1949–August 17, 1950
September 10, 1967–March 28, 1969
April 21, 1986–November 8, 1987

LESSON FOR REACHING POTENTIAL: Relax! Being stressed all the time will only give you tension headaches. You will be just as successful without aggravating yourself.

HEALTH: Get outside. Play, run, ski, climb mountains.

MOST IMPORTANT LIFE LESSON: The expression of courage, honesty, and integrity.

GENERAL ATTITUDE SHOULD BE: "I'm here, and I'm ready for the world to recognize my talents!" "I'm passionate about everything and want to experience all that life has to offer, but I will stay humble."

DOMESTIC ATTITUDE MIGHT BE: "I've been faced with heavy domestic responsibilities, usually at an early age. However, I'm independent, and often have to throw my weight around, but I will always try to be considerate."

ROMANTIC ATTITUDE MIGHT BE: Since your greatest love lessons include the testing of your fidelity and your ability to stay passionate and honest, your attitude might be: "It's not that difficult to keep me happy! Just don't let me become bored. Let's have fun together."

SOUL MATES: Greatest soul mate compatibility comes with Libra, Gemini and Aquarius.

HOW TO SUCCESSFULLY LINK UP WITH YOUR SOUL MATE: Let your magnetic, athletic prowess shine and be a love-magnet. Walk, bike, jog with a large, friendly dog.

YOUR MOST SUCCESSFUL CAREER PATH: Your challenge is to express yourself in a superior manner, but not to insensitively roll over other people. "I want to shine and be recognized for my abilities, but in the process, I don't want to hurt others." Entrepreneur, computer whiz, politician, artist, member of the military.

YOUR GREATEST KEY TO YOUR WEALTH AND PROSPERITY: Greatest life lessons involve your desire to be financially successful and to achieve that prominence. The key is doing it with morality and virtue. "I'm wealthy, and I deserve it!"

KEY TO YOUR SUCCESSFUL AND PERMANENT WEIGHT LOSS: Use this affirmation three times a day for the rest of your life, letting it flow deeply into your consciousness: "Less of me, Dear Lord, and more of you, will permanently bring about the weight loss that will help me to be healthy, strong, and attractive. Thank you for your support and guidance."

LIFE GOALS: Success and prosperity.

YOUR GREATEST LIFE CHALLENGE: To be able to express your greatest abilities, yet be able to stay humble.

Soul Potential—PISCES
May 27, 1913–December 13, 1914

January 7, 1932–July 25, 1933
August 18, 1950–March 7, 1952
March 29, 1969–October 15, 1970
November 9, 1987–May 28, 1989

LESSON FOR REACHING POTENTIAL: Don't let the world pass you by. Your mysticism and sensitivity can put you at a slight disadvantage.

HEALTH: Wear great shoes!

GENERAL ATTITUDE: "Is this real, or is it my imagination? Am I living in a dream world?"

DOMESTIC RELATIONSHIPS: "I will not allow addictions or any of my fantasy dreams and wishes to interfere with the way I interact with my children."

ROMANTIC RELATIONSHIPS: "I will make sure that I do not become bored in relationships. I will use my imagination, and include my partner in my fantasy world. I will suggest that they share their fantasies with me as well."

SOUL MATE: Best soul mate match is born under the sign of Virgo, Taurus, or Capricorn.

HOW TO SUCCESSFULLY LINK UP WITH YOUR SOUL MATE: Best way to link up with a soul mate is in an atmosphere involved either with the healing arts, or in a theatrical or film setting.

YOUR MOST SUCCESSFUL CAREER PATH: Any of the healing professions are ideal, notably chiropractic, massage therapy, nursing, or medical arts.

YOUR GREATEST KEY TO LASTING WEALTH AND PROS-PERITY: Use your intuition in all of your life pursuits. For example, if you go into real estate or the healing arts, use your ESP to discern what the issues really are. Your natural discernment will insure your success and keep you prosperous. With regard to money, find a financial counselor to work with you.

YOUR GREATEST KEY TO SUCCESSFUL AND PERMANENT WEIGHT LOSS: Use this affirmation three times a day for the rest of your life, letting the words flow deeply into your consciousness: "Less of me, Dear Lord, and more of you will permanently bring about the weight loss that will help me to be healthy, strong, and attractive. Thank you for your support and guidance."

GREATEST LIFE CHALLENGE: Keeping it real.

DAILY MEDITATION AND AFFIRMATION FOR YOUR GREATEST SOUL GROWTH AND PSYCHIC DEVELOP-MENT:"I am tuned in to the highest and best in the universe. I will use my intuition to bring me the best that the universe has to offer. I give thanks, I give thanks, and I give thanks!"

Soul Potential—AQUARIUS
December 14, 1914–July 2, 1916
July 26, 1933–February 12, 1935
March 8, 1952–October 2, 1953
October 16, 1970–May 5, 1972
May 29, 1989–December 15, 1990

LESSON FOR REACHING POTENTIAL: Keep your feet firmly planted on the ground. Remember, charity begins at home.

HEALTH: You are not being a hypochondriac when you take care of health issues. Don't ignore regular check-ups.

GENERAL ATTITUDE: "I love everyone and everyone loves me."

DOMESTIC RELATIONSHIPS: "I have to remember that charity begins at home. I can't neglect my family for the needs of strangers."

ROMANTIC RELATIONSHIPS: "I must remind myself that I may have universal love for all mankind, but my greatest happiness will probably come with the exchange of love with just one person."

SOUL MATE: Your North Node draws you into soul-mate relationships with people born under the sign of Leo, Aries, or Sagittarius.

HOW TO SUCCESSFULLY LINK UP WITH YOUR SOUL MATE: Charitable endeavors, such as volunteering your time for worthy organizations or in spiritual groups of service, will link you up with that special soul mate.

YOUR MOST SUCCESSFUL CAREER PATH: Most North Node Aquarians love working in a service-oriented career where they feel they are needed. For instance, nursing, massage therapy, optometry, but also in careers that are involved with advanced space, scientific, or technical involvements.

YOUR GREATEST KEY TO LASTING WEALTH AND PROSPERITY: Don't let your generous heart and spirit allow you to pour your financial security down the drain. Make sure that the friends and associates, that you so generously treat, will appreciate your kindness; and keep things in a fair and balanced situation.

YOUR GREATEST KEY TO SUCCESSFUL AND PERMANENT WEIGHT LOSS: Use this affirmation three times a day for the rest of your life, letting it flow deeply into your consciousness: "Less of me, Dear Lord, and more of you will permanently bring about the weight loss that will help me to be healthy, strong, and attractive. Thank you for your support and guidance."

GREATEST LIFE CHALLENGE: Discernment. Knowing how to spend your time, money, and energy, so that it is not squandered.

DAILY MEDITATION AND AFFIRMATION FOR YOUR GREATEST SOUL GROWTH AND PSYCHIC DEVELOPMENT: "I will meditate daily, and listen carefully to what I am hearing, sensing, and feeling. I will put the members of my immediate family ahead of people who indicate that they need me, or want to be with me."

Soul Potential—CAPRICORN

July 3, 1916–January 19, 1918
February 13, 1935–September 1, 1926
October 3, 1953–April 12, 1955
May 6, 1972–November 22, 1973
December 16, 1990–July 4, 1992

LESSON FOR REACHING POTENTIAL: "All work and no play, makes Jack a dull boy."

HEALTH: Take time to walk in the sun. Play, even though it doesn't come naturally for you. Your health will prosper. No more headaches!

GENERAL ATTITUDE: "If I work twenty-four hours a day, seven days a week, and save every penny, everything will be fine."

DOMESTIC RELATIONSHIPS: Be careful. Your children may want more of *you*, and less financial security.

ROMANTIC RELATIONSHIPS: Don't be so cheap. It will only hurt your love life.

SOUL MATE: Your best soul mate is born under the sign of Cancer, Scorpio, or Pisces.

HOW TO SUCCESSFULLY LINK UP WITH THAT SOUL MATE: Many people who have the North Node in Capricorn meet their soul mate in financial institutions, such as in a bank, or in online banking. In addition, in any atmosphere connected to computer technology.

YOUR MOST SUCCESSFUL CAREER PATH: North Node Capricorns are successful when working with computer technology or in the teaching field.

YOUR GREATEST KEY TO LASTING WEALTH AND PROSPERITY: Learn to invest your money wisely, to help it increase your holdings and wealth. In other words, think *big*! Financial security and prosperity is not achieved with just hard work and hoarding. Wise investments and real estate involvements can also work well for you.

YOUR GREATEST KEY TO SUCCESSFUL AND LASTING WEIGHT LOSS: Use this affirmation three times a day for the rest of your life, letting it flow deeply into your consciousness: "Less of me, Dear Lord, and more of you will permanently bring about the weight loss that will help me to be healthy, strong, and attractive. Thank you for your support and guidance."

GREATEST LIFE CHALLENGE: The greatest challenge of North Node Capricorn people is usually learning to trust that the universe will bring them everything and anything that they need. You don't always have to expend great effort or the sweat of your brow.

DAILY MEDITATION AND AFFIRMATION FOR YOUR GREATEST SOUL GROWTH AND PSYCHIC DEVELOPMENT: "I will work hard, but I will also know when to stop and rest. I will make sure that there is enough time in my life for love, sex, laughter, fun, and recreation. Life is short!"

CHAPTER 9: KEY 4

Initiate the Karmic Shift

Life's challenges are karmic situa-tions. These situations are in place to alter unconstructive attitudes and characteristics. For every lingering karmic situation, an unfavorable attitude is responsible.

Many of life's circumstances are far from easy or from how we imagined. They are far from perfect, in fact. Loving families? Stimulating, lucrative careers? Pleasure–filled, emotionally–charged love relationships? These aren't supposed to be just the stuff of paperback fiction, they are supposed to be yours to have and hold forever—right?

The truth is that "perfect" is not just one thing. What may be perfect for you on the soul's level isn't so on another. The level we're talking about here, of course is the conscious one. The one that thinks and feels and knows the difference between pleasure and pain. The one you care about. Talk of the soul's "development" is fine and all that, but the fact is, what the soul may or may not need doesn't necessarily fit in with your plans right now. Your conscious plans, that is, the way you want things, are what's important. So, what do you do? How do you "shift" into the more constructive attitude? Let me explain.

When things are not going well, some of us are still filled with hope and optimism that the something "better" is just around the bend, while others feel constricted, negative, hurt, or downright hopeless. And when tragic life circumstances happen, all bets are off. We feel run–over, run–down, out of control, shocked, betrayed, desperate, depressed, hopeless, and much less than alive. These difficult and painful experiences force us through a "bounce–back" period, or a mourning period, where we need to adjust emotionally to new circumstances. This bounce-back period can occur over the course of a few hours, a few days, weeks—as in a breakup in a relationship or career setback—or in the case of tragedy, months and years. Sometimes, it can occur in a period of minutes. The bounce-back allows us to return with a new outlook, and with some sense that we have to return to the "living." At its very best, this period causes us to grow in some way we had not previously adequately addressed. At its very worst, it can engulf us in misery so profound that we lose all hope, faith, and respect for life.

How do we recognize these situations which are supposedly in place for our "growth" if that's in fact what they are? How do we recognize them as karmic situations, and not some unfair joke of the universe? If they are "karmic," then why on Earth can't we just avoid these situations and go straight to the learning without them? Why do we need to go through a complicated divorce or battle over the children, or (God forbid) lose a loved one to illness or some freak accident, or to struggle endlessly in a dead-end career because you desperately need the money?

The answer is that life's challenging circumstances awaken us. They awaken us either in an extreme, moderate, or extremely slight sense; by brutally quick circumstance, by subtle occurrence, or through lingering, seemingly endless struggle.

A friend of mine, let's call her Annabelle, completely holistic in every sense of the word, in a loving marital relationship, has a child with severe emotional disabilities. The strain that dealing with this child has put on all factors of her life is debilitating, if not downright crippling. At times, she has confided, she feels like ramming her car into a tree, or at the very least putting her son on the medicines she has sought so hard to avoid. During her emotional lows she has sought out the comfort of friends, chocolate, and even starting and quitting smoking. Each setback and every emotional crisis takes its toll, yet each time she survives the bounce-back period with a resiliency that is amazing. Through it all she is asking *why*? *Why* is this happening to us? *What* are we to be learning about our relationships, what am *I* to be learning about the place of myself in my child's world, *what* am I to be gaining from this experience—or giving to the other parties involved?

It is a true quest, and the answers are not easily found. But bit by bit she is surviving and adjusting. Who knows where it will lead? Along the way, Annabelle and her husband are being forced to change their relationship dynamic in many ways, making concessions, and altering their family structure in order to deal with the emotional needs of this child. So how is this relevant? It is obvious to this friend that the situation her family finds themselves in is karmic, because their relationships are taking on new changes; their attitudes are shifting, and in a sense—although how is still to be determined—it is an awakening.

This is what defines a karmic situation: an experience which is forcing some shift in our lives, relationships or attitudes—whether we recognize that shift or not.

How many of us have come through a relationship break-up only to find that we are stronger or in some way changed? How many of us have come through the experience of a death or long illness of someone we love and come away unchanged? Even the smallest of experiences can be karmic. A five-dollar bill found on the street and pocketed, then being caught by a watching child—how does this make you feel? Do you react by lying: "I was just picking it up so I could find the owner . . . "? Or by telling the truth? Or do you get embarrassed and slink off? A small act, with a small result, maybe. Or maybe a large result, if you stop to think about it.

What you could do now, is get out pen and paper, and after looking further down the page, list as many situations that are currently happening to you, or in which you find yourself, that you feel might be karmic experiences—that are causing a shift, or some kind of change in your personality, thinking, or circumstance. Your notes are only for your use.

Here's "Annabelle's list," that my friend mentioned before:

Physical distance from my larger family causing me to stand up on my own
Emotional distance from immediate family—what is this doing to all of us?
Son's emotional problems/needs overtaking everything else
Husband and love relationship—can it survive?
Career difficulties, at an impasse, nowhere to go

Once you have written down your issues, read through the following list, separated into categories. Think about how any of these may apply to yourself or someone very close to you.

CHALLENGES LIST

PARENTING/CONCEPTION/BIRTH
Easy conception, birth, upbringing
Close, harmonious relationships
Emotional struggles
Control issues
Lack of respect
Early childhood illness
Infertility
Adoption
Abortion
Overly fertile
Miscarriage
Arguments and hostility
Birth abnormalities
SIDS (sudden infant death syndrome)

RELATIONSHIPS
Happy, loving partnership
Occasional struggles
Control issues
Emotional neediness
Unable to find, keep, or attract the right partner
Unable to commit or a tendency to over–commit
Unable to say no
Abusive
Victimized
Unfaithful
Unable to love
Unable to feel
Indifference

Emotional indifference
Physical indifference

SEXUALITY
Loving and fulfilling sexuality
Good, when you have it
Never good
Never have it
Frigidity
Cheating
Promiscuity
Lack of passion
Gender confusion
Sadism
Machismo
Homosexuality
Bisexuality
Transsexuality
Fear of intimacy
Reluctance for intimacy
Afraid to reveal body

PHYSICAL HEALTH/APPEARANCE
Physical attractiveness
Extreme beauty
Dislike of appearance
Extreme unattractiveness
Overweight
Too thin
Too tall
Too short
Obesity
Physical malformation
Physical impairment
Blood problems
Allergies
Skin problems

Arthritis
Back problems
Joint problems
Chronic illness
Eye and vision problems
Respiratory problems
Birth defects
Paralysis
Smoking
Drug use
Alcoholism

LIFE PATH
Fulfilling, successful career choice
Emotionally torn over career choice
Stress–filled job
Huge material gain
Emotional lack of fulfillment
"Something missing"
Lack of material gain
Lack of career permanence
Job despair
Lack of direction
Uncertainty
Trouble with superiors
Boredom
Lack of ambition
Career fluctuation
Disillusionment
Lack of hope
Dead–end career
Waiting for retirement
Waiting for something better

EMOTIONAL/PSYCHOLOGICAL/MENTAL MANIFESTATION
Alzheimer's disease
Bulimia

Anorexia
Depression
Anxiety
Hostility
Mood swings
Paranoia
Claustrophobia
Mental disorders
OCD, including emotional eating
Mental illness
Substance abuse

More of these apply than you had expected, don't they? But you don't need to worry. The purpose of going through this list is to flag areas of your life which are undergoing change for karmic reasons.

These areas can be broken down into:
Lessons of the Mind
Lessons of the Body
Lessons of the Spirit

All are intertwined, and are leading us to the same place: harmonious balance, unconditional love for ourselves and others, and self-realization. As Yogananda says, "God created each man [and woman] as a soul, dowered with individuality, hence essential to the universal structure, whether in the temporary role of pillar or parasite. His freedom is final and immediate, if he so wills; it depends not on outer but inner victories." *Autobiography of a Yogi*, chapter 16

CHAPTER 10: KEY 5

Remove Harmful Attitudes

*By determining what you are sup-*posed to gain from your attitudes, you are moving toward eliminating those attitudes that prolong or create negative situations.

To understand which of these circumstances may have gotten (or are getting) the better of us, and may become negative areas of constriction—creating feelings of negativity, loss, hopelessness, confusion, or apathy—the underlying tendencies must be found. These tendencies are attitudes delaying the completion of the bounce-back period, turning it into a negative and potentially harmful area—harmful to your own emotional well-being, and possibly to those around you.

These attitudes, once identified, must be broken through and re-established in the positive. All characteristics can turn into a nonproductive hindrance, or in the extreme, debilitating and harmful. The idea is to reestablish balance by turning personality "stumbling blocks" into enabling characteristics. This may seem oversimplified, but in truth many of our life difficulties boil down to the way we approach (or avoid) our problems.

The following list identifies underlying attitudes—emotional conditions resulting from the situations in which you have found yourself. These cause problems to linger, reoccur, and ultimately—if not resolved—to become conditions which can handicap your life.

Take a look at the list and recognize the attitudes or emotional conditions you find yourself in. To do this properly, you must be in a quiet room. Do not rush yourself, or attempt this when you will be called away. Concentrate on each attitude and carefully assess whether it applies to you. Bare-naked truth is what is called for here—no subterfuge, and no denial. If you can do this quickly, you may not be getting at the truth. If you feel you simply can't do this, then ask a close friend for help. Make sure this friend has no ulterior motive or jealousies, or it won't work. If you still feel unable to adequately attempt this step, learn meditation techniques and get at the part of your consciousness which is hiding itself from you.

Expose those attitudes which are intensifying negative situations, so you can move your karma along. Tick off those attitudes that apply, or jot them down. You'll need them for reference for the next step.

ATTITUDES, CONDITIONS, AND TENDENCIES
Abusive lifestyle
Acting only to please
Absorbing negative thoughts of others
Acting out inappropriate sexual behavior
Actions based on fear or lack
Addictive behavior
Addictive habits
Addictive, violent, dark, brooding emotions
Addiction
Alienation
Alienation from female organs/femininity
Aloof, withdrawn
Ambivalence about sexual identity or gender
Alienated from mother or from mothering
Ambivalent feminine creativity especially between career and home
Anemic
Anger
Anguish
Anxiety hidden by a mask of cheerfulness
Apathy
Argumentative
Arrogance

Asceticism (severe simplicity)
Aversion to the bodily self
Avoidance of commitment
Avoidance of emotional pain
Avoidance of reality
Avoidance of the present
Avoidance of traumatic or painful events/personal aspects
Awkward awareness of body

Bitterness
Burdensome dutifulness
Burned-out feeling

Chaotic inner life
Childish dependency
Chronic dissatisfaction
Complete exhaustion after a long struggle
Co-dependence
Confusion
Confusion about feminine creativity, especially between career and
home
Confusion about life direction
Confusion about sexual identity or gender
Conflict with authority
Conflicting motives
Constricted feelings
Creating barriers
Criticalness
Cutting, sharp

Daydreaming
Deception
Deep fear or terror
Deep fear of sexuality and intimacy
Deep fears
Deeply repressed emotions
Defensiveness

Demanding
Denial of emotional pain
Denial of the spiritual world
Depletion of life force and emotional verve
Depression
Desire to escape self-awareness
Despair
Destroyed sense of self
Destructive impulses
Difficulty saying no
Disconnection after shock or trauma
Disconnection from inner voice
Disconnection from marital responsibility
Disconnection from self, from others
Discouragement
Disdain of social relationships
Disgust toward the bodily self
Disorientation
Distant
Distorted sense of self
Distorted connection with the masculine self
Disturbed dreams, sleep
Dominated by others
Domineering
Doubt or self-doubt
Drug addiction
Dull heaviness
Dull or "hung over"
Dull, sluggish
Dulling the consciousness through drugs, alcohol
Dysfunctional in group settings
Dysfunctional relationships

Easily distracted
Easily depleted
Easily influenced
Easily influenced by family ties

Easily overwhelmed
Easily panicked due to group thought
Easily upset
Emotional attachment to the past
Emotional imbalance
Emotional repression
Emotional tension
Emotional trauma stored deep within body
Envy
Escapism
Escape through drugs, overeating, and alcohol
Excessive ambition
Excessive masculine (yang) forces
Exhaustion
Expectation of failure
Extreme dependency and emotional regression
Extreme vulnerability to others and the environment

Failure to acknowledge one's own light and uniqueness
Failure to learn from experiences
False states of emotionality
Fanaticism
Fatigue
Fear (relationships based on)
Fear of aging
Fear of being violated
Fear of death
Fear of deep feelings
Fear of everyday life
Fear of exposure
Fear of intense feeling
Fear of intimacy
Fear of losing control
Fear of mortality
Fear of parenthood
Fear of reaching out to others
Fear of rejection

Fear of retribution or censure if one departs from religious conventions
or family community
Fear of sexual intimacy
Fear of the occult or spiritual experience
Fear of the unknown
Fearful anticipation
Feeling cut off from love
Feeling cut off from spirit
Feeling persecuted
Feeling powerless
Feeling that sex is impure
Feeling rejected
Feeling ugly or rejected because of personal appearance
Feeling unclean
Feeling unequal to the task required
Feeling unwanted
Feeling victimized
Feeling weighed down
Feelings of childhood abandonment, abuse
Feelings of shame, guilt, unworthiness

Generalized depression
Giving up on life
Gloom
Greed and lust for possessions and power
Guilt

Habits which undermine or circumvent true intention of self
Hard-driving
Hardened, cut-off
Heaviness
Helplessness
Hesitation
Hidden fears of spiritual world
Hiding essential self from others
Hopelessness
Hostile attitude

Hostile, distant
Hypersensitivity to environment

Identification with youth and lower personality
Immaturity
Impatience
Imposing will on others
Impractical ideals
Inability to acknowledge one's own uniqueness
Inability to accept oneself
Inability to be assertive
Inability to be true to yourself
Inability to bring creative forces into expression
Inability to connect with one's female sexuality
Inability to cope with deep feelings
Inability to experience human warmth in sexual experiences
Inability to feel quiet inner presence or attunement
Inability to form bonds with social community
Inability to give freely and openly
Inability to integrate higher purpose with real life and work
Inability to gain wider perspective
Inability to give freely
Inability to hear one's higher voice
Inability to make change
Inability to meditate or pray
Inability to move forward
Inability to perceive higher purpose and meaning in life events
Inability to put goals and ideals into concrete action
Inability to release emotional tension
Inability to resolve issues of anger and powerlessness
Inability to speak clearly
Inability to stay centered in body
Inability to take a stand
Inability to take inner responsibility for one's healing
Inability to take responsibility
Inability to take straightforward action
Inappropriate sexual behavior

Indecisiveness
Indecision about life direction
Infidelity
Inflated spirituality
Inflation of self or unbalanced sense of individuality
Inflexible
Inner conflicts about sexuality
Insecurity
Insensitivity to the sufferings of others
Iron-willed
Irritable
Irritation
Isolation
Intensification of pain and suffering due to isolation
Internalized grief
Intolerance
Invalidating what one knows

Jealousy
Judgmental

Lack of assertiveness
Lack of awareness of the consequences of one's actions
Lack of commitment or focus
Lack of confidence
Lack of emotional clarity
Lack of hope
Lack of humor
Lack of life force
Lack of support from father
Lack of trust in higher providence
Lack of vitality in expression
Lack of physical warmth, vitality
Lacking creativity
Lacking inner strength
Lacking inspiration
Leadership distorted by self-aggrandizement

Lethargy
Lingering illness
Listlessness
Loneliness
Longing for what was
Low self-esteem
Low self-worth
Low vitality
Lying

Marital stress
Masking one's feelings
Materialism
Melancholia
Mental lethargy
Midlife crisis
Mistrust
Moody

Needy
Negative behavior
Nervous exhaustion
Nightmares
Nostalgic longing
Not feeling at home on the earth
Numbing of the emotions accompanied by mechanization or hardening
of the body

Obsessed with imperfection
Obsessive fear or worry for others
Obsessive compulsion to cleanse
Obsessive worry
Out of touch with physical world
Over-absorbent of negative influences
Overactive psychic life, out of touch with physical world
Overbearing behavior
Overburdened

Over-concerned with one's own problems
Over-dependence on words of others
Over-involvement in psychic or religious
Over-identification with personal appearance
Over-influenced by beliefs or values of family or community
Over-influenced by past events
Over-intellectualization of reality
Overcome with personal needs and desires
Overcome with pessimism, despair
Over-dependence on external help for physical ailments
Overly aggressive, competitive
Overly delicate
Overly dry, intellectual
Overly masculine aspect of self
Overly scientific
Overly self-protective activities
Overly serious
Overly talkative
Over-striving
Overly tense
Overly somber sense of self
Overwhelmed by details
Overwhelmed by duties and responsibilities
Overwhelmed by too many ideas
Overwhelmed due to over-stimulation

Paranoid
Perceiving life as ill-fated or undeserved
Perfectionist expectations
Physical awkwardness
Physical toxicity
Poor relationship to father or masculine self
Possessive love
Possessiveness
Preoccupation with mediumship
Preoccupation with personal appearance
Preoccupied with personal needs and desires

Procrastination
Profound feeling of alienation
Profound melancholia
Profound shyness, reserve
Protective of personal boundaries
Psychic contamination
Psychic vulnerability
Psychosomatic illness
Pushing beyond one's limits

Rejection of female organs/femininity
Repeating mistakes
Repressed emotions
Repressed inner child
Repressed or misdirected libido
Repressed sexual feelings
Repression of emotions
Repression of trauma or painful situations
Resentful
Resignation
Rigid standards for oneself

Seeing life in bits and pieces rather than as whole
Seeking outside oneself for false forms of light or knowledge
Self-absorbed
Self-blame
Self-censorship
Self-centeredness
Self-criticism
Self-deception
Self-denial
Self-destructive
Self-effacement
Self-neglect
Self-pity
Self-protection
Sense of alienation

Separation of sexuality from moral behavior
Separatist tendencies
Servile
Sexual depletion
Sexual imbalance
Sexual repression
Shattered by trauma or abuse
Shock or trauma from recent or past experience
Shyness
Socially insecure
Speech impediments
Spiritual pride
Stagnation
Stress
Strong despair, anguish
Subject to peer pressure, social obligation
Suppression of traumatic or painful events
Suppression of traumatic or painful events from childhood
Susceptible to mass hysteria and panic
Suspicion

Tendency to hysteria or emotionality
Tension
Tension around jaw
Threatened by physical or emotional closeness
Trauma stored within body
Tyrannical

Unable to accept oneself
Unable to bear life's circumstances
Unable to communicate with others
Unable to concentrate
Unable to cope with simultaneous events
Unable to stand for one's convictions
Unable to trust higher providence
Uncertainty of oneself
Unfocused thought

Unworthiness

Vacillation in the face of challenge
Vague anxiety
Verbal aggression and hostility

Wandering, seeking
Wavering between two choices
Weak–willed
Weariness
Weighed down by the mundane
Weighed down, depressed
Withdrawal
Withdrawal in the face of challenge
Worrisome repetitive thoughts

If you are questioning your own soul's growth, that is terrific, and a normal part of human evolution. We are the sum of all our parts: emotional, physical, mental, and spiritual. We are the product of our experiences, in this life and those in the past, and on top of that each of us is on our individual life path. We all suffer from emotional trauma brought about by life conditions, influenced as we have said, by the patterns mapped at our birth, determined by where we have come from and where we are going. The key is to work through these attitudes for greater understanding and growth, not to feel bad or to deny having them.

CHAPTER 11: KEY 6

Change Your Emotional Condition

Hopefully, in completing this next step you will have at least one AHA! moment. Those are the flashes of insight when something becomes suddenly clear; the clouds break away, and an instant of crystal–clear perception, understanding, or relief occurs. It's okay to cry, hiss, or shout: "Hey, I am normal, this is why this is happening!" or to just let out a long, slow, "Oooooh!"

Take out your lists and use them to find the appropriate entries in the Karmic Dictionary, which reveals where your attitudes should be leading, and the change in emotional condition that is necessary to liberate yourself.

Karmic Dictionary

Abusive lifestyle: Bravery to meet head–on rather than draw back from harmful or negative situations

Acting to please: Internal strength, acting with purpose, refusing others when appropriate

Absorbing negative thoughts: Strength and clarity of thought, mental integrity, and positivity

Addictive behavior: Emotional honesty, obtaining true inner peace

Addictive habits: Sparkling vitality, awake and refreshed, in touch with life

Alienation: Spirituality, cosmic consciousness, and caring

Alienation from female organs/femininity: Acceptance of one's femininity, deepened experience of the female body

Alienation from male organs/masculinity: Acceptance of one's masculinity, deepened experience of the male body

Aloof, withdrawn: Perceptive sensitivity, elevated spiritual perspective, sharing with others while remaining true to self; sharing one's gifts with others, appreciation of social relationships

Ambivalence about sexual identity or gender: Clarity about sexual identity, self-acceptance, balance of feminine and masculine qualities

Alienated from mother or from mothering: Maternal consciousness, warm, feminine nurturing, mother–child bonding, healing of the inner child

Ambivalent feminine creativity especially when torn between career and home: Warmhearted feminine creativity, productive nurturing

Anemic: Earthly vitality

Anger: Feeling love and extending love to others, universal compassion, open heart, emotional honesty, direct and clear communication of strong emotions

Anguish: Deep courage and faith that comes from knowing and trusting the spiritual world

Anxiety hidden by a mask of cheerfulness: Emotional honesty, obtaining true inner peace

Apathy: Love for the earth and for human life, enthusiasm for doing and for serving

Argumentative: Healing warmth and receptivity, especially in the use of the spoken word

Arrogance: balanced sense of individuality, spiritualized ego forces, sun–radiant personality

Asceticism: flexibility, spontaneity, flowing with the spirit rather than the letter of the law

Aversion to the bodily self: Integration of the spiritual self into physical world

Avoidance of commitment: Awareness of, and healing of, painful earlier memories, ability to respond emotionally and form deep, committed relationships

Avoidance of emotional pain: Emotional honesty, obtaining true inner peace

Avoidance of reality, or of the present: Awake focus, manifesting inspiration in everyday life

Avoidance of traumatic or painful events/personal aspects: Awake consciousness, penetrating insight

Awkward awareness of body: Grace-filled movement, physical and etheric harmony

Bitterness: acceptance, forgiveness, taking responsibility for one's life situation, flowing with life

Burdensome dutifulness: charismatic leadership, contagious enthusiasm, joyful service

Burned-out feeling: Balanced and centered creative activity

Chaotic inner life: balanced psychic awareness, deep penetration and understanding of the transpersonal aspects of oneself

Childish dependency: Healthy maturation, acceptance of responsibilities

Chronically dissatisfied: work as an expression of inner calling; outward life which expresses one's true goals and values, work experiences motivated by an inner sense of life purpose

Complete exhaustion after a long struggle: Revitalization through connection with one's inner energy

Co-dependence (relationships based on): Loving others unconditionally with an open heart, emotional freedom

Confusion: decisiveness, inner resolve, acting from the certainty of inner knowing

Confusion about life direction: work as an expression of inner calling; outward life which expresses one's true goals and values, work experiences motivated by an inner sense of life purpose

Confusion about sexual identity or gender: clarity about sexual identity, self-acceptance, balance of feminine and masculine qualities

Confused focus between career and home: warmhearted feminine creativity, productive nurturing

Conflict with authority: a sacred sense of tradition and lineage, ability to learn from elders

Conflicting motives: Pure clarity of purpose, sincerity

Constricted feelings: Free–flowing emotions, capacity to express a full range of human emotions, especially pain and sadness

Creating barriers: Warm and personable, open–hearted friendliness

Criticalness: Tolerance, acceptance of other's differences and imperfections, seeing the good within

Cutting, sharp: Healing warmth and receptivity, especially in the use of the spoken word

Daydreaming: Awake focus, manifesting inspiration in everyday life

Deception: Strong sense of inner conscience, truthfulness, uprightness

Deep fear, terror: Self–transcending courage, inner peace and tranquility when facing great challenges

Deep fear of sexuality and intimacy: Balanced integration of human warmth and sexual intimacy, ability to express deep feelings of love and connectedness in sexual relationships

Deep fears: Illumined consciousness, light–filled awareness and strength

Defensiveness: Innocence and trust

Demanding: Selfless love given freely, respecting the freedom and individuality of others

Denial of emotional pain: Emotional honesty, obtaining true inner peace

Depression: Positive and optimistic feeling about the world and future events, sun–like forces of caring, encouragement, and purpose

Desire to escape self–awareness: Healthy ego strength, independence, self–reliance

Despair: Emotional equanimity, finding joy in life

Destroyed sense of self: Core integrity, maintaining an integrated sense of self even when severely challenged

Destructive impulses: Spiritual surrender and trust, feeling protection and guidance from higher power, balance and equanimity despite stress

Difficulty saying no: Serving others from inner strength, acting from inner purpose, saying no when appropriate

Disconnection after shock or trauma: Conscious embodiment, recovery from deep–seated shock or trauma

Disconnection from marital responsibility: Polarization of sexual from the spiritual

Discouragement: Abiding faith and hope, light-filled optimism

Disdainful of social relationships: Sharing one's gifts with others, appreciation of social relationships

Disgust toward the bodily self: Integration of the spiritual self into physical world

Disorientation: Alignment with the earth, grounded presence, calmness and stability

Distant: Emotional openness and vulnerability, ability to be close with others

Distorted connection with the masculine self: Loving strength, balance of masculine and feminine energy

Distorted sense of self: Balanced sense of individuality, spiritualized ego forces, sun-radiant personality

Disturbed dreams, sleep: Balanced psychic awareness, deep penetration and understanding of the transpersonal aspects of oneself; illumined consciousness, light-filled awareness and strength

Dominated by others: Serving others from inner strength, acting from inner purpose, saying no when appropriate

Domineering: Selfless service, tolerance for the individuality of others

Doubt: Perseverance, confidence, faith to continue despite setbacks

Drug addiction: Balanced psychic awareness, deep penetration and understanding of the transpersonal aspects of oneself

Dulling the consciousness through drugs, alcohol: Healthy ego strength, independence, self-reliance

Dullness: Inspired creativity, deep soulfulness in touch with higher realms, radiant vision and perspective, precise thinking, disciplined focus and concentration

Dysfunctional in group settings: Harmonious social consciousness, finding higher identity in a group, flexibility

Dysfunctional relationships: Loving awareness of others, appropriate emotional boundaries

Easily distracted: Precise thinking, disciplined focus and concentration

Easily depleted: Inner radiance and strength of aura, compassionate awareness, inclusive sensitivity, beneficent healing forces

Easily influenced: Strength from active resistance, individuality, sense of balance

Easily overwhelmed: Active consciousness, alert, flexible, and mobile state of mind

Easily panicked: Calm steady presence, especially in emergency situations

Easily upset: Serene, sun–like disposition, emotional balance

Emotional attachment to the past: Being fully in the present, learning from the past while releasing it

Emotional imbalance: Spiritual insight and vision, integration of psychic faculties with emotional aspect of self

Emotional repression: Awareness of and healing of painful earlier memories, ability to respond emotionally and form deep, committed relationships

Emotional trauma: Serene, sun–like disposition, emotional balance

Envy: Feeling love and extending love to others, universal compassion, open heart

Escapism: Finding spirituality within, developing an inner center of knowing

Escape through drugs, overeating, and alcohol: Healthy ego strength, independence, self–reliance

Excessive ambition: Altruistic sacrifice of personal desires for common good, inner purity

Excessive yang forces: Cooperative service with others, extending feminine forces in social situations, inner peace and harmony as a foundation for relationships

Exhaustion: Lively creativity, artistic activity

Expectation of failure: Self-confidence, creative expression, spontaneity

Extreme dependency and emotional regression: Healthy ego strength, independence, self–reliance

Extreme vulnerability to others and the environment: Inner radiance and strength of aura, compassionate awareness, inclusive sensitivity, beneficent healing forces

Failure to learn from experiences: Learning the lessons of life experience, understanding the laws of karma, wisdom

False states of emotionality: Emotional vitality, ability to express deep feelings

Fanaticism: Ability to practice moderation, tolerance, balance, finding the middle-ground

Fatigue: Energy, enthusiasm, involvement in life's tasks

Fear (relationships based on): Loving others unconditionally with an open heart, emotional freedom

Fear of aging: Shifting ego identification from self to higher spiritual identity, feeling oneself as transpersonal and transcendent

Fear of being violated: Emotional openness and vulnerability, ability to be close with others

Fear of death: Spiritual surrender at death or times of deep transformation; self-transcending courage, inner peace, and tranquility when facing great challenges

Fear of intense feeling: Emotional honesty, direct and clear communication of strong emotions

Fear of intimacy: Emotional openness and vulnerability, ability to be close with others

Fear of losing control: Spiritual surrender and trust, feeling protection and guidance from higher power, balance and equanimity despite stress

Fear of mortality: Shifting ego identification from self to higher spiritual identity, feeling oneself as transpersonal and transcendent

Fear of parenthood: Awareness of and healing of painful earlier memories, ability to respond emotionally and form deep, committed relationships

Fear of reaching out to others: Warm and personable, open-hearted friendliness

Fear of rejection: Emotional honesty and openness, courage to take emotional risks

Fear of retribution or censure if one departs from religious conventions or family community: Inner calm and clarity when experiencing spiritual contact, the courage to trust and discern, love-based spirituality

Fear of sexual intimacy: Balanced integration of human warmth and sexual intimacy, ability to express deep feelings of love and connectedness in sexual relationships

Fear of the occult or spiritual experience: Inner calm and clarity when experiencing spiritual contact, the courage to trust and discern, love-based spirituality

Fear of the unknown: Trust and confidence to meet the unknown, drawing inner strength from spiritual world

Fearful anticipation: Caring for others with calm inner peace, trust in the unfolding of life events

Feeling cut off from love: Feeling love and extending love to others, universal compassion, open heart

Feeling cut off from spirit: Feeling protection and guidance from spiritual beings

Feeling persecuted: Inner fortitude despite outer hardship, perseverance

Feeling powerless: Emotional honesty, direct and clear communication of strong emotions

Feeling that sex is impure: Inner purity of the soul, sexual and spiritual integration

Feeling rejected: Awareness of and healing of painful earlier memories, ability to respond emotionally and form deep, committed relationships

Feeling ugly or rejected because of personal appearance: Beauty that radiates from within, self-acceptance

Feeling unclean: Inner sense of purity

Feeling unequal to the task required: Joyous service, faith and confidence to complete task

Feeling victimized: Acceptance, forgiveness, taking responsibility for one's life situation, flowing with life

Feeling weighed down: Inspired creativity, deep soulfulness in touch with higher realms, radiant vision and perspective

Feelings of childhood abandonment, abuse: Maternal consciousness, warm, feminine nurturing, mother-child bonding, healing of the inner child

Feelings of shame, guilt, unworthiness: Emotional honesty and openness, courage to take emotional risks

Generalized depression without obvious cause: Emotional equanimity, finding joy in life

Giving up on life: Will to live, joy in life

Gloom: Emotional equanimity, finding joy in life

Greed and lust for possessions and power: Selfless service, altruistic sacrifice of personal desires for common good, inner purity

Guilt: Self-acceptance, self-forgiveness, freedom from inappropriate guilt or blame

Habits which undermine or circumvent to true intention of self: Decisive and goal-oriented, deliberate purposeful action, self-directed

Hard driving: Effortless energy, lively activity balanced with inner ease

Hardened, cut-off: Sensitive and receptive attunement, serene inner listening to others and higher worlds, especially in dreams or meditation

Heaviness: Buoyant courage and optimism

Helplessness: Healthy maturation, acceptance of responsibilities

Hesitation: Decisiveness, inner resolve, acting from the certainty of inner knowing

Hidden fears: Trust and confidence to meet the unknown, drawing inner strength from spiritual world

Hiding essential self from others

Hopelessness: Abiding faith and hope, light-filled optimism

Hostile attitude: Cooperative service with others, extending feminine forces in social situations, inner peace and harmony as a foundation for relationships

Hostile, distant: Emotional openness and vulnerability, ability to be close with others

Hypersensitivity to environment: Absorbing the fullness of life especially in its sensory aspects

Identification with youth and lower personality: Shifting ego identification from self to higher spiritual identity, feeling oneself as transpersonal and transcendent

Immaturity: Healthy maturation, acceptance of responsibilities

Impatience: Patient acceptance, flowing with life and with others

Imposing will on others: Selfless service, tolerance for the individuality of others

Impractical ideals: Awaken focused, manifesting inspiration in everyday life

Inability to acknowledge one's own uniqueness: Radiant self-light unattached to outward recognition or fame

Inability to accept oneself: Self-acceptance, self-forgiveness, freedom from inappropriate guilt or blame

Inability to be assertive: Articulate and colorful in verbal expression, active dynamic projection of oneself in social situations

Inability to be true to yourself: Well-developed individuality, inner sense of balance

Inability to bring creative forces into expression: Lively creativity, artistic activity

Inability to connect with one's female sexuality: Warmth and responsiveness in female sexuality, integration of soul warmth and bodily passion

Inability to cope with deep feelings: Peace centered in heart, integration of physical and emotional well-being through harmonious connection with the earth

Inability to experience human warmth in sexual experiences: Balanced integration of human warmth and sexual intimacy, ability to express deep feelings of love and connectedness in sexual relationships

Inability to feel quiet inner presence or attunement: Sensitive and receptive attunement, serene inner listening to others and higher worlds, especially in dreams or meditation

Inability to form bonds with social community: Commitment to community, social connectedness, a sense of one's place on Earth

Inability to gain wider perspective: Cosmic overview and perspective

Inability to give freely: Generous and inclusive, a giving and sharing nature, feeling inner sense of abundance

Inability to hear one's higher voice: Strong sense of inner conscience, truthfulness, uprightness

Inability to meditate or pray: Sensitive and receptive attunement, serene inner listening to others and higher worlds, especially in dreams or meditation

Inability to move forward: Fiery, energetic, capable of change, and transformation

Inability to perceive higher purpose and meaning in life events: Drawing wisdom from life experience. Reviewing one's life process from higher perspective

Inability to put goals and ideals into concrete action: Clearly directed forces of will, decisive action

Inability to release emotional tension

Inability to resolve issues of anger and powerlessness

Inability to speak clearly, to be assertive: Articulate and colorful in verbal expression, active dynamic projection of oneself in social situations

Inability to stay centered in body: Alignment with the earth, grounded presence, managing diverse forms of activity

Inability to take a stand: Forthright masculine energy, warrior-like spirituality that confronts and transforms

Inability to take inner responsibility for one's healing: Healthy vital sense of self, healing and beneficent forces rising within, deep sense of wellness and wholeness

Inability to take responsibility: Healthy maturation, acceptance of responsibilities

Inability to take straightforward action: Decisive and goal-oriented, deliberate purposeful action, self-directed

Inappropriate sexual behavior: Balanced integration of human warmth and sexual intimacy, ability to express deep feelings of love and connectedness in sexual relationships

Indecisiveness: Strong sense of inner conscience, truthfulness, uprightness; decisiveness, inner resolve, acting from the certainty of inner knowing

Indecision about life direction: Work as an expression of inner calling; outward life which expresses one's true goals and values, work experiences motivated by an inner sense of life purpose

Inflated spirituality: Expansive spirituality, meditative insight

Inflation of self: Balanced sense of individuality, spiritualized ego forces, sun-radiant personality

Inflexible: Balanced strength, accepting limits, knowing when to surrender; acceptance, forgiveness, taking responsibility for one's life situation, flowing with life

Insecurity: Feeling at home in the world

Insensitivity to the sufferings of others: Empathy, receptive to the feelings of others, acting from inner truth and guidance

Iron-willed: Balanced strength, accepting limits, knowing when to surrender

Irritable: Serene, sun like disposition, emotional balance

Irritation: Patient acceptance, flowing with life and with others

Isolation: Becoming involved in the world, sharing one's gifts with others, awareness of connections in ones relationships, soul-based relationships

Intensification of pain and suffering due to isolation: Transcendent consciousness, finding the larger meaning in such suffering, compassionate awareness and attention to the meaning of pain and suffering

Internalized grief: Free-flowing emotions, capacity to express full-range of human emotion, especially pain and sadness

Intolerance: Tolerance, acceptance of other's differences and imperfections, seeing the good within, patient acceptance, flowing with life and with others; ability to practice moderation, tolerance, balance, finding the middle-ground

Invalidating what one knows: Trusting one's own inner knowing, intuition, self-confidence, and certainty

Jealousy: Feeling love and extending love to others, universal compassion, open heart

Judgmental: Tolerance, acceptance of other's differences and imperfections, seeing the good within

Lack of assertiveness: Forthright masculine energy, warrior-like spirituality that confronts and transforms

Lack of awareness of the consequences of one's actions: Empathy, receptive to the feelings of others, acting from inner truth and guidance

Lack of commitment or focus: Work as an expression of inner calling; outward life which expresses one's true goals and values, work experiences motivated by an inner sense of life purpose

Lack of confidence: Buoyant courage and optimism, creative expression, spontaneity

Lack of emotional clarity: Loving awareness of others, appropriate emotional boundaries

Lack of hope: Will to live, joy in life

Lack of humor: Free-flowing emotions, capacity to express full-range of human emotion, especially pain and sadness

Lack of life force: Glowing vitality, radiant energy and warmth

Lack of support from father (during childhood): Childlike innocence and trust, feeling at home in the world, at ease with oneself, supported and loved, connected

Lack of trust in higher providence: Generous and inclusive, a giving and sharing nature, feeling inner sense of abundance

Lack of warmth, vitality (due to prior exploitation or abuse): Warmth and responsiveness in female sexuality, integration of soul warmth and bodily passion

Lacking inner strength: Becoming involved in the world, sharing one's gifts with others

Lacking inspiration: Inspired creativity, deep soulfulness in touch with higher realms, radiant vision and perspective

Lacking physical warmth: Warm physical presence, vibrant

Leadership distorted by self-aggrandizement: Charismatic leadership, contagious enthusiasm, joyful service

Lethargy: decisive and goal-oriented, deliberate purposeful action, self-directed

Lingering illness: Will to live, joy in life

Listlessness: Earthly vitality, precise thinking, disciplined focus and concentration

Longing for what was: Being fully in the present, learning from the past while releasing it

Loneliness: Awareness of connections in ones relationships, soul-based relationships

Low self-esteem: Balanced sense of individuality, spiritualized ego forces, sun-radiant personality

Low self-worth: Radiant self-light unattached to outward recognition or fame

Low vitality: Strength from active resistance, exuberant artistic activity

Lying: Strong sense of inner conscience, truthfulness, uprightness

Masking one's feelings: Emotional honesty and openness, courage to take emotional risks

Materialism: Holistic thinking, perceiving life with spiritually clear thought; altruistic sacrifice of personal desires for common good, inner purity

Marital stress: Integration of sexuality and spirituality

Melancholia: Transcendent consciousness, finding the larger meaning in suffering, compassionate awareness: Emotional equanimity, finding joy in life

Mental lethargy: Mindfulness, wakeful clarity, mental alertness

Midlife crisis: Shifting ego identification from self to higher spiritual identity, feeling oneself as transpersonal and transcendent

Moody: Serene, sun like disposition, emotional balance

Needy: Selfless love given freely, respecting the freedom and individuality of others, also: Healthy maturation, acceptance of responsibilities

Negative behavior (to gain attention): Selfless love given freely, respecting the freedom and individuality of others

Nervous exhaustion: Integration of spiritual purpose with daily work, spiritualized sexuality, and grounded spirituality, bringing spiritual power into the root chakra

Nervous exhaustion from over striving: Ability to practice moderation, tolerance, balance, finding the middle-ground

Nightmares: Trust and confidence to meet the unknown, drawing inner strength from spiritual world

Nostalgic longing: Being fully in the present, learning from the past while releasing it

Not feeling at home on Earth: Humanized spirituality, cosmic consciousness warmed with caring for all that is human and earthly

Numbed emotions: Peace centered in heart, integration of physical and emotional well-being through harmonious connection with the earth

Obsessed with imperfection: An inner sense of purity

Obsessive fear or worry for others: Caring for others with calm inner peace, trust in the unfolding of life events

Obsessive compulsion to cleanse: Deep awareness of the inner self, capable of transformation and change

Obsessive worry: Cosmic overview and perspective

Out of touch with physical world: Integrating psychic or dream experiences into daily life, multidimensional consciousness

Over–absorbent of negative influences: Inner radiance and strength of aura, compassionate awareness, inclusive sensitivity, beneficent healing forces

Overbearing behavior: Ability to practice moderation, tolerance, balance, finding the middle–ground

Overburdened: Energy, enthusiasm, involvement in life's tasks

Over–concerned with one's own problems: Inner tranquility, emotional self-sufficiency

Over–dependence on words of others: Trusting one's own inner knowing, intuition, self–confidence, certainty

Over–involvement in psychic or religious: Healthy spirituality; opening, balanced psychic and physical openings, grounded presence in everyday life

Over–identification with personal appearance: Beauty that radiates from within, self-acceptance

Over–influenced by beliefs or values of family or community: Freedom from limiting influences, making healthy transitions in life, courage to follow one's path or destiny

Over–influenced by past events: Freedom from limiting influences, making healthy transitions in life, courage to follow one's path or destiny

Over–intellectualization of reality: Holistic consciousness, synthesizing ideas into wholeness

Overcome with personal needs and desires: altruistic sacrifice of personal desires for common good, inner purity

Overcome with pessimism, despair: Positive and optimistic feeling about the world and future events, sun–like forces of caring, encouragement, and purpose

Over–dependence on external help for physical ail–

ments: Healthy vital sense of self, healing and beneficent forces rising within, deep sense of wellness and wholeness

Overly aggressive, competitive: Loving strength, balance of masculine and feminine energy; cooperative service with others, extending feminine forces in social situations, inner peace and harmony as a foundation for relationships

Overly delicate: Becoming involved in the world, sharing one's gifts with others

Overly dry, intellectual: Glowing vitality, radiant energy and warmth

Overly scientific: Holistic thinking, perceiving life with spiritually clear thought

Over–seriousness: Childlike humor and playfulness, experiencing the joyful inner child, lightheartedness

Over–talkative: Inner tranquility, emotional self–sufficiency

Over–striving: Effortless energy, lively activity balanced with inner ease

Over–tense: Effortless energy, lively activity balanced with inner ease

Overly somber sense of self: Free-flowing emotions, capacity to express full range of human emotion, especially pain and sadness

Overwhelmed by details: Active consciousness, alert, flexible, and mobile state of mind

Overwhelmed by duties and responsibilities: Joyous service, faith, and confidence to complete task

Overwhelmed by too many ideas: Integration of ideas and speech, ability to express thoughts with clarity

Overwhelmed due to over–stimulation (sensory congestion): Absorbing the fullness of life especially in its sensory aspects

Paranoid: Loving inclusion of others, positive expectation of goodwill from others, ability to trust

Perceiving life as ill–fated or undeserved: Drawing wisdom from life experience; reviewing one's life process from higher perspective

Perfectionist expectations: Tolerance, acceptance of others' differences and imperfections, seeing the good within

Poor relationship to father or masculine self: Balanced

sense of individuality, spiritualized ego forces, sun–radiant personality

Possession: Strength and clarity of thought, mental integrity, and positivity

Possessive love: Selfless love given freely, respecting the freedom and individuality of others

Possessiveness, (relationships based on): Loving others unconditionally with an open heart, emotional freedom

Preoccupation with mediumship: Healthy spiritual; opening, balanced psychic and physical openings, grounded presence in everyday life

Preoccupation with personal appearance: Beauty that radiates from within, self–acceptance

Preoccupied with personal needs and desires: altruistic sacrifice of personal desires for common good, inner purity

Procrastination: Decisive and goal–oriented, deliberate purposeful action, self–directed

Profound feeling of alienation: Humanized spirituality, cosmic consciousness warmed with caring for all that is human and earthly

Profound shyness, reserve: Highly perceptive sensitivity, elevated spiritual perspective, sharing with others while remaining true to self

Psychic contamination: Strength and clarity of thought, mental integrity, and positivity

Psychic vulnerability: Illumined consciousness, light–filled awareness, and strength

Psychosomatic illness: Emotional vitality, ability to express deep feelings

Pushing beyond one's limits: Balanced strength, accepting limits, knowing when to surrender

Repeating mistakes: Learning the lessons of life experience, understanding the laws of karma, wisdom

Repressed emotions: Free–flowing emotions, capacity to express full range of human emotion, especially pain and sadness

Repressed inner child: Free–flowing emotions, capacity to express full-range of human emotion, especially pain and sadness

Repressed or misdirected libido: Lively dynamic energy, communication that is emotionally balanced

Repressed sexual feelings: Balanced integration of human warmth and sexual intimacy, ability to express deep feelings of love and connectedness in sexual relationships

Repression of emotions: Emotional honesty, direct and clear communication of strong emotions

Repression of trauma or painful situations: Awaken consciousness, penetrating insight

Resentful: Acceptance, forgiveness, taking responsibility for one's life situation, flowing with life

Resignation: Abiding faith and hope, light-filled optimism; will to live, joy in life

Rejection of female organs/femininity: Acceptance of one's own femininity, deepened experience of the female body

Resignation: Love for the earth and for human life, enthusiasm for doing and for serving

Rigid standards for oneself: Flexibility, spontaneity, flowing with the spirit rather than the letter of the law

Seeing life in bits and pieces rather than as a whole: Holistic consciousness, synthesizing ideas into wholeness

Seeking outside oneself for false forms of light or knowledge: Finding spirituality within, developing an inner center of knowing

Self–absorbed: Inner tranquility, emotional self–sufficiency

Self–blame: Self-acceptance, self-forgiveness, freedom from inappropriate guilt or blame

Self–censorship: Self-confidence, creative expression, spontaneity

Self–centeredness: Selfless love given freely, respecting the freedom and individuality of others

Self–criticism: Self-acceptance, self-forgiveness, freedom from inappropriate guilt or blame

Self–deception: Strong sense of inner conscience, truthfulness, uprightness

Self–denial: Flexibility, spontaneity, flowing with the spirit rather than the letter of the law

Self-effacement: Balanced sense of individuality, spiritualized ego forces, sun-radiant personality

Self-neglect: Serving others from inner strength, acting from inner purpose, saying no when appropriate

Self-pity: Inner fortitude despite outer hardship, perseverance

Self-protection: Becoming involved in the world, sharing one's gifts with others

Sense of alienation from past: Awareness of what is ancient and sacred, ability to learn from elders

Separation of sexuality from moral behavior: Integration of sexuality and spirituality

Separatist tendencies: Cooperative service with others, extending feminine forces in social situations, inner peace, and harmony as a foundation for relationships

Servile: Serving others from inner strength, acting from inner purpose, saying no when appropriate

Sexual depletion: Integration of spiritual purpose with daily work, spiritualized sexuality, and grounded spirituality, bringing spiritual power into the root chakra

Sexual imbalance: Spiritual insight and vision, integration of psychic faculties with sexual aspect of self

Sexual repression: Awareness of and healing of painful earlier memories, ability to respond emotionally and form deep, committed relationships

Shattered by trauma or abuse: Core integrity, maintaining an integrated sense of self even when severely challenged

Shock or trauma resulting from recent or past experience: Bringing soothing, healing qualities, a sense of inner divinity

Socially insecure: Warm and personable, open-hearted friendliness

Speech impediments: Articulate and colorful in verbal expression, active dynamic projection of oneself in social situations

Spiritual pride: Expansive spirituality, meditative insight

Stagnation: Fiery, energetic, and capable of change and transformation

Stress: Alignment with the earth, grounded presence

Strong despair, anguish: Deep courage and faith that comes from knowing and trusting the spiritual world

Subject to peer pressure, social obligation: Well-developed individuality, inner sense of balance

Suppression of traumatic or painful events from child-hood: Releasing painful memories

Susceptible to mass hysteria and panic: Calm steady presence, especially in emergency situations

Suspicion: Feeling love and extending love to others, universal compassion, open heart

Tendency to hysteria or emotionality: Integrating psychic or dream experiences into daily life, multidimensional consciousness

Tension: Patient acceptance, flowing with life and with others

Tension around jaw: Lively dynamic energy, communication that is emotionally balanced

Trauma stored within body: Grace-filled movement, physical and etheric harmony

Tyrannical: Selfless service, tolerance for the individuality of others

Unable to concentrate: Precise thinking, disciplined focus and concentration

Unable to cope with simultaneous events: Active consciousness, alert, flexible and mobile state of mind

Uncertainty of oneself: Trusting one's own inner knowing, intuition, self-confidence, certainty

Unfocused thought: Integration of ideas and speech, ability to express thoughts with clarity

Vacillation in the face of challenge: Forthright masculine energy, warrior-like spirituality that confronts and transforms

Vague anxiety: Trust and confidence to meet the unknown, drawing inner strength from the spiritual world

Verbal aggression and hostility: Lively dynamic energy, communication that is emotionally balanced

Violent, dark emotions: Courage to confront rather than retreat from abusive or threatening situations

Wandering, seeking: Commitment to community, social connectedness, a sense of one's place on the earth

Wavering between two choices: Decisiveness, inner resolve, acting from the certainty of inner knowing

Weakness: Strength from active resistance

Weak–willed: Serving others from inner strength, acting from inner purpose, saying no when appropriate

Weariness: Energy, enthusiasm, involvement in life's tasks

Weighed down by the mundane: Holistic thinking, perceiving life with spiritually clear thought

Weighed down, depressed: Positive and optimistic feeling about the world and future events, sun–like forces of caring, encouragement and purpose

Withdrawal: Becoming involved in the world, sharing one's gifts with others

Withdrawal in the face of challenge: Forthright masculine energy, warrior–like spirituality that confronts and transforms

Withdrawn: Sharing one's gifts with others, appreciation of social relationships

Worrisome repetitive thoughts, chattering minds: Inner quiet, calm, clear mind

CHAPTER 12: KEY 7

Apply the Lessons of Your Life

After reading through the Karmic Dictionary in the previous chapter, you should be able to isolate the emotional conditions behind your patterns and unwanted circumstances.

These emotional conditions have been distilled into 27 major categories that you will find below. One or more may be causing you difficulty.

Find the underlying emotional condition and the solution for each Life Lesson. Write the lesson on index cards and place them where you will see them throughout the day. Absorb this and other lessons you have learned here, and work them into every facet of your life.

Emotional Conditions and Their Lessons

ANGER/HOSTILITY

He that is slow to anger is better than the mighty; he that ruleth his spirit better than he who taketh a city.—Anonymous

Anger is one of the most destructive influences of and on the mind.
LESSON: Control, love, and empathy

CONDEMNATION
A double-edged sword, highly destructive. Jesus said, "Let he who is without fault cast the first stone." Recognize your own flaws; only when you are perfect may you move on to others' flaws
LESSON: Love and recognize the unconditional worth of others.

CRITICAL DESTRUCTIVENESS
It is the inferior person who needs to be superior to others
LESSON: Recognize worth in others

DECEIT
Deceit rebounds with self-condemnation and lack of self-esteem. It results in imbalances of body and mind.
LESSON: Love yourself and others enough to not deceive them

HYPOCRISY
Physiological ills are often a direct result of guilt and cloaked behavior. Guilt can kill you.
LESSON: Truthfulness in all things

FEAR
Humankind's enemy, the root of many problems. Excise it from your soul.
LESSON: Stimulus to action.

GREED/ACQUISITIVENESS
Jesus asked, "What would it profit you to gain the whole world and lose your own soul?" Spiritual growth is more valuable than all the material possessions we might acquire.
LESSON: Realignment of values

HATRED
Look for the underlying fear then excise it. Do not cast your negative emotions upon others; they have the same right to learn as you do even if they have caused you great harm. Replace hatred with a desire to find the God-power within the persons you despise. Hatred

engenders hatred, love begets love.
LESSON: Forgiveness, trust, unselfish love

HOPELESSNESS
Nothing happens by chance; rather, there is a divine nature to all things. Everything happens so that we may move upward in the eternal progress of life.
LESSON: Trust

HYPERSENSITIVITY
Having to do with an individual's sense of importance and wounded pride.
LESSON: Offense at any slight is a negative impulse, real or imagined

IMPATIENCE
Indiscriminate action breeds fear, discouragement, irritability, and ultimately self-condemnation.
LESSON: Tolerance, action, and faith

INABILITY TO GIVE OR RECEIVE LOVE
Love is the most powerful spiritual force in the universe, expressing the greatest qualities of the soul. True love, which comes from the Creator, is untainted by jealousy, possession, lack of trust, or selfishness. This lack is often caused by repeated disappointments in love, or growing up in an environment with too little loving expression.
LESSON: As the Master said, "Love one another as I have loved you."

IRRITABILITY
A subtle form of anger which over a period of time is capable of harm to the physical body.
LESSON: There are choices in life; stay rational

JEALOUSY
Highly negative impulse causing harm to yourself and others.
LESSON: Trust in others and in infinite wisdom

LACK OF ASPIRATION
Lack of hope, or slipping backwards, in reality or in one's mind.
LESSON: Openness to new promise or ideals

LACK OF COURAGE
Caused by disappointment, belief in one's failure.
LESSON: Loyalty, devotion, and commitment

LACK OF EMPATHY
Compassion for the distress and suffering of others is vital in the soul's growth.
LESSON: We are our brothers' keepers.

LACK OF FAITH
Lack of faith is caused by disappointment and discouragement; when it becomes part of one's personality it can result in bitterness and confusion, and ultimately in grave physical imbalances. There is order in the universe; disaster on the face of it may look like disaster but there is often an underlying spiritual cause, a higher lesson to be learned, a place to go from there. If you despair not, your pain will come to an end.
LESSON: Trust in the divine nature of things.

LACK OF FORGIVENESS
"Forgive them Father, they know not what they do," said Jesus. The inability to forgive oneself or others clutches negativity to the heart, usually resulting in illness.
LESSON: Universal love

LACK OF KINDNESS
Rise above greed, hatred, jealousy, or envy.
LESSON: We feel less sorry for ourselves when we respond to the needs of others

PREJUDICE/INTOLERANCE
Dwelling on insignificant details or petty annoyances is the opposite of genuine understanding. "Judge not, lest ye yourself be judged."
LESSON: You are falling backwards on the path to soul growth and enlightenment

PRIDE/BOASTFULNESS/SELF–CENTEREDNESS

Qualities which retard the development of the soul.

LESSON: Recognize worth in others, not be so quick to boast about your own

SELF–CONDEMNATION

Another worthless emotion, unless it is followed with a plan for not repeating past mistakes.

LESSON: Love yourself, forgive

SELFISHNESS

The opposite of kindness and generosity, a form of self–protection, of fear. "And though I have the gift of prophecy and understand all the mysteries, and all the knowledge; and though I have all faith, so that I could remove mountains, and have not charity, I have nothing." Truly, we must do unto others as we would have them do unto us.

LESSON: "Bread cast upon the waters will be returned threefold in time."

VANITY

The need for recognition and approval.

LESSON: Self-worth comes from inside

WORRY

A worried, troubled mind causes illness to manifest in the body. Worry accomplishes nothing.

LESSON: Positive action

Levels Of Mastery

The lessons of life are moving us all toward the center, into an integrated whole—not only integrated and whole individuals, but integrated families, communities, countries, and planet.

Emotional truth, bravery
leads to
Sexual, interpersonal attunement

leads to
Unconditional love, emotional strength
leads to
Knowledge, wisdom of the larger scheme of things
leads to
Attunement with the earth, nature, and one another
leads to
Spiritual acceptance, flowering
leading to
Physical, mental, spiritual balance
leads to
Full integration (the center) as individuals,
communities, and mankind

Part III

Life Lessons

The events of childhood do not pass, but repeat themselves like seasons of the year.
Eleanor Farjeon

You have not chosen me but I have chosen you.
John 15:16

CHAPTER 13

How We Are Conceived

Choosing Our Parents

One of the most commonly asked questions regarding reincarnation is about whether we choose our parents, and if so, why? The answer, which is of course, yes, happens to shed light on the concept of karma.

We do choose our parents. Yet it isn't merely the parents that we select, but the lifestyle, personalities, and experience a particular family offers. This is a selection over which our angels hold particular influence. There may be many sets of parents who are attractive to the incoming entity, and it is only with the angels' help that the right ones are chosen. Even though we may be completely unhappy with our parents—and at one time or another most of us have felt this way—ours are the correct parents for our soul's karmic needs.

Angels are able to access the Akashic records and to note an entity's past deeds, intent and experiences. When it's the soul's turn to come into a physical body, a great deal of effort and co-ordination is involved. Should the entity be born to a single mother? Should it be adopted? Should there be two devoted, loving parents? The possibilities are carefully explained to the entity. A lifetime of easy karma, comfort, and affluence, may offer little opportunity for growth or challenge. A lifetime of difficult karma, however, may be just what the soul needs to balance previous experiences, and proceed at an accelerated pace.

Being born into poverty to a single mother, may, for example, work out unfinished karma of a lifetime of selfishness. There may be a physical handicap, such as a short leg and a limp, to help work out the karma from the lifetime as a soldier when the entity took pleasure in maiming and killing. The problem with this soul was not that he killed, but with his attitude of enjoying the suffering of others. This is not in keeping with the universal law of love and compassion. Since at the time of his death the entity had still not learned compassion or mercy, his is considered to be unfinished karma.

While the angels of the Akashic records are patiently explaining to the protesting entity why he needs a life of deprivation rather than one of luxury, the birth experience might actually be occurring. This would explain why so many babies are born howling.

Sometimes, we're almost magnetically drawn to a certain set of parents because they're so much like us. In my case, my father was a pharmacist. As a young child I delighted in spending hours in his drugstore. Sitting on a counter stool, I would watch with great fascination as he prepared prescriptions with his mortar and pestle. When he let me help him count capsules, I thought he was the best father a person could possibly have.

Anything parents have not learned from experience, they can now learn from their children.—Anonymous

Through meditation and past-life regression, I have since learned of lifetimes as a small-town doctor, an Indian medicine man, a Chinese herbalist and acupuncturist, and as a nun who was a nurse. Of course I was at home amid the pharmacopoeia of a drugstore.

The mother I chose was absolutely right for me. A psychic and astrologer in her own right, she directed me to develop my own psychic abilities and stimulated my love for all things esoteric. She gave me fascinating insight into astrology, dream analysis, graphology, and many other—what were at the time unconventional—areas.

My mother never cared that most preschoolers were not interested in esoteric subjects. As young as I was, three or four years old, she would call me in to her bedroom, sit me on her bed and ask, "Joy, what do you think this means? I dreamt I was sitting at the edge of a dock fishing." When I offered something along the lines that she must have been looking for something important, she replied, "That's great! Of course! It means that I am looking for wisdom, as represented by the water, and the Christ within, as shown by the desire to catch fish. According to the laws of symbology, fish usually represents Christ. Thank you, Honey, that was so helpful."

My mother taught me to read before I started school. I didn't think that was strange at all, nor that the reading primer with which she taught me was *Zolar's Book of Astrology, Numbers and Dreams*. She never failed to convince me that everything I did was wonderful and that there was anything that I couldn't do.

My mother also proved to me that you could "read" or analyze just about anything if you needed answers. When she drained pasta, for example, she would often grow excited and say,

"Joy, come quickly! Look at this!"

I would reply, "What, Ma?"

And she would say, "Look at the message in the bottom of this spaghetti pot. Look how the spaghetti is stuck to the bottom. Can you see it? Here's your cousin Carole, and there's a baby in her arms. At last! She'll be so happy after all the miscarriages."

My mother was so psychic that she could find accurate messages in just about anything. She was fun, and through her I learned many metaphysical and practical truths. Yet growing up was traumatic. I felt isolated as a child, and was forced to take care of myself at a very young age. My mother was physically handicapped and had to depend on others, particularly me, to complete tasks that were normally done by adults. This was doubly difficult, since my father was stricken with repeat illnesses. My existence was surrounded by curious and frightening sicknesses—ambulances in the middle of the night, waiting rooms, and hours of not knowing whether my father was going to recover from another one of his heart attacks, or if my mother would be succumbing to one of her debilitating bouts of asthma.

Yet, my overexposure to sickness, doctors, and hospitals, opened my eyes to the insufficiencies of medical science, and made me receptive to holistic medicine, and the healing powers within.

Yes, I would say that my parents were just about perfect for me.

In *The Case for Reincarnation*, Joe Fisher relates the story of Romy Crees, a toddler from Des Moines, Iowa. As soon as she could talk the little girl insisted she was "Joe Williams of Charles City, husband of Sheila and father of three children." After she described her gory death in a motorcycle accident, her parents were jolted into taking action. Giving in to her desire to "go home they took her to Charles City, where they met Mrs. Williams at the home in which she raised her late son, Joe Williams. All was as Romy described, also identifying the people in the old woman's photographs.

"She recognized them," murmured Mrs. Williams, incredulously, "she recognized them!"

Sometimes saturation occurs after many lifetimes of following the same patterns. Finding our parents difficult to get along with, or even repugnant, may cause us to realize that we have to move out of the patterns we have been following with them. Other times it is a simple balance for previous lifetimes spent together.

Many people, usually until they have matured into adulthood, are unable to accept that they may have chosen their parents. It would be wise for young people to give the concept some consideration. It would shed light on their family problems and explain a great deal.

Dr. David Chamberlain, in *Babies Remember Birth*, recounts the results of birth regressions, one of which was Sarah, not long after she had been born:

> I'm not a baby. I'm not any age . . . I've known them. I don't understand why they keep acting like they have just known me this short time. I'm really frustrated . . . I'm supposed to be in charge. I know they named me Sarah because Sarah means princess. They knew who I was, that's how come they named me Sarah. I wish they would remember, because the more they treat me this way, the harder it is for me to remember who I am. I just don't want them to be in charge, and I can't seem to explain to them . . . they don't understand.

When We Are Born

Before the birth experience many souls enter and leave or "visit" the developing embryo or fetus. This coming and going can occur up to six months after birth. Sometimes it happens that a soul will enter the embryo at conception and stay for a lifetime. On other occasions, no soul will stay within the fetus, unable to find the experience or vibratory level compatible with his needs. When this coincides with the parents needing that particular karmic experience, a stillbirth or miscarriage can occur.

In my own case, I felt the presence of my daughter's soul hovering near me before birth. She came in at the moment of delivery, and never left. With my younger child, Scott, I felt his soul enter at the time of quickening, or when I first felt movement of him as a fetus. Yet I was aware that he often came and went before being born. He made a special point of leaving my body whenever I played the guitar. First he would give me a couple of kicks, and then he'd be gone.

I was reminded of Scott's comings and goings years later when as a teenager, he sat listening to me strum my well-worn guitar. He had become an accomplished musician by then, and the distress on his face was palpable.

"Ma, why don't you take lessons?" he suggested pointedly. That was his gentle way of saying that I've always needed guitar lessons, but never took the time and trouble to have any musical training. He was a talented musician, even before he was born.

> Think no thoughts which should not have entry into a child's soul.—Rudolf Steiner

Abortion

A soul has to be born at the right time, in addition to being born to the proper parents and place. Can you imagine the cosmic work that's involved in a challenge like that? When an entity takes his first breath, he is astrologically programmed for life, within an ethereal grid that stays with him for that entire lifetime. This grid indicates the lessons to be learned and to what degree. This pattern can be read in the aura, or the individual's electric field. Since astrological patterns contain all past, present, and future karmic indications, it is essential that the person be born at the precisely correct moment in time, and to the right parents.

> The night before one of my patients had a spontaneous abortion, she shouted herself awake several times, yelling, "I want to get out, let me out!

She is convinced that it was her unborn child speaking through her.—Thomas Verny, M.D., *Secret Life of the Unborn Child*

With so much going into the birth process, one might conclude that the act of aborting a fetus entails serious karmic repercussions. It's true that abortion should never be taken lightly, nor used as a method of birth control. For in addition to karmic implications for the parent, the incoming soul will feel a jarring sense of rejection and lack of love. While this may be an experience that the aborted being requires—the soul may not have understood the full implications of abortion when they were themselves in a physical body, for example—it is not an excuse for parents to act callously.

Abortion may occur when one or both parents lack faith. This may be a lack of faith in themselves, or in the Creator, or in what the universe is able to supply. This lack of faith, coupled with fear, creates the foundation for abortion.

After abortion, the incoming entity is usually given a choice. It can be redirected to another set of parents, or born to the same mother at a later date. This choice is also given to entities who are miscarried, stillborn, or die in infancy. The angels are truly aware of all that occurs on the earth, and nothing goes unnoticed or neglected. All things in time—not necessarily our time, but perhaps in the time of the angels.

When abortion is a consideration, I recommend the following:

Pray for the correct guidance, so that the outcome will be in keeping with God's will, and for the greater good of all concerned.

Meditate, and listen for whatever answer and guidance comes. Give yourself a day or two to think about it, and allow yourself to be guided by God.

If you do choose the path of abortion, enter into it with the greatest of reverence. Ask for God's grace and forgiveness, and offer love to the rejected entity, asking too for its forgiveness and understanding. Tell this soul that you hope for a rejoining at a later time, when it will be better for all concerned.

Abortion is a perfect example of how we are given the gift of free will. It's a choice that we should have and exercise with the greatest of care and discernment.

We should have the greatest respect for the Creator's gift of life. Whatever we do should not be done out of selfishness. Only upon reflection of what is in your heart can you determine what is actually "selfish." Perhaps putting the sanctity of marriage before having another child would not be selfish, if you feel the strain on your marriage would be intolerable. Only you can make that determination.

Do what you do without guilt and with full awareness, discernment, and inner guidance. Remember that depression sets up a pattern of self-destruction, which provides a foundation for poor mental health and illness. Guilt is always wrong.

Miscarriage, Stillbirth, Crib Death

Sometimes the body of the fetus is genetically deformed or possesses such physical problems that no incoming soul is willing to take the body. Even if the karma is meant to be dealt with by that soul, it may be too daunting at that particular time. This may result in miscarriage, stillbirth, or infant death.

Incoming souls are given a period of six months after birth to make the decision of whether to stay or leave the physical body. When they leave, it is usually identified as crib death, or SIDS (Sudden Infant Death Syndrome), since in most instances there is no physical cause for death. Whether pulling out of the body or staying, it is done on deep subconscious levels.

In the situation of SIDS, the incoming entity, along with its angels, may decide that the parents or environmental conditions are not right for the soul's greatest growth. Perhaps the situation in which the soul finds itself is too easy, or too difficult. Although drawn to, for example, loving parents, siblings, financial comfort, and a beautiful home, upon closer inspection the soul might realize that the situation does not offer enough challenge or opportunity for growth.

Dr. Verny's studies led him to a report from Dr. Peter Fedor-Freybergh, one of Europe's leading obstetricians, who described the birth of 'Kristina:'

> Although robust and healthy, Kristina steadfastly refused her mother's breast after birth, and for days afterward. Another nursing mother offered to try the child at her own breast, and Kristina eagerly grasped and sucked it for all it was worth. "Why

do you suppose the child reacted that way?" he asked the mother.

She didn't know.

"Was there illness during your pregnancy?"

"None," the mother replied.

"Well, did you want to get pregnant then?"

The woman looked up at him and said, "No, I didn't. I wanted an abortion. My husband wanted the child. That's why I had her."

Kristina had been shut out emotionally in the womb and now, barely four days old, she was determined to protect herself from her mother any way she could.

Difficulty Conceiving, Infertility

Sometimes infertility indicates misplaced priorities in this lifetime or in one previous. Not paying attention to the "biological clock," being too busy building a career, know that if your body says conceive at 17 or 18, and your career says 30 or 40, it's still only a matter of time before the eggs stop dropping.

In her book *Out on a Limb*, Shirley MacLaine describes her relationship with her mother as "strained." While in New Mexico, undergoing acupuncture for past-life regression, she understood why the relationship wasn't better. She relived an experience where her mother, who wasn't her mother at the time, left her to die in a desert.

When I was in my twenties I could actually feel my eggs come down the fallopian tube—a split second of shooting pain and it goes down—and by the time I grew older felt fewer and fewer eggs, then no eggs coming down. So I knew when I was no longer fertile. But by then I had had my children, too early perhaps, and I didn't have to worry about the tick, tick, ticking.

The concept here is timing: make karma work for you. Nature wants you to make a choice, to use your discernment, to work with nature and not against it. Sometimes procreation means compromise, work, awareness of one's body and a little thing called "reality." If you marry an individual in his fifties, chances are his sperm count is going to be on the low side. If you are in your mid-thirties when you have children, as so many of us are these days, realize that your body is not going to be as adept at making babies as someone in their twenties.

Infertility can be a tremendous learning-and-growth experience, particularly when it occurs over a lengthy period of time. A friend of mine tried to conceive for more than ten years, and underwent all sorts of tests and fertility treatments, against the advice of those who said it was physically impossible because of a pre-existing medical condition. But Patsy *knew* she would be a mother, and that the children would be her own. At last Patsy defied the odds and naysayers and conceived triplets. Then out came the naysayers again with their voices of doom—the triplets were underweight; she and they were at risk; they would never be carried to term without serious injury to mother and children, and so on. As she heard these horror stories for six months her conviction wavered. Finally, she came back to the confidence that these children would be healthy, and this gave her the strength to not schedule an early C-section at six months, as the doctors advised. Instead she followed her conscience, her intuition, a strict and natural diet plan, and found a new doctor with a reputation for delivering healthy multiple-birth babies at term. She then, indeed gave birth to three healthy baby boys, at term. Today, they have broken the charts for triplets, larger and more boisterous than most single-birth babies their age. But for ten years while Patsy and her husband tried to conceive and then attempted to carry to term a risky pregnancy, they went from knowing little more than the basics of conception, to being so well informed about fertility and multiple births that they could teach a college course.

In addition to the learning experience for the parents, the three happy souls who came in were not meant to be born a decade earlier, but at those moments, on that day, in that year. As a result everyone grew from the experience, learning among other things, to trust their own inner guidance and not blindly accept the advice which was offered them.

> You may give them your love but not your thoughts,
> For they have their own thoughts.
> You may house their bodies but not their souls,
> For their souls dwell in the house of tomorrow,
> Which you cannot visit, not even in your dreams.
> ——Kahlil Gibran, *The Prophet*

Adoption

Some parents need the experience of raising children born to some-body else, perhaps balancing the act of giving up one's own children at another time. So too, the birth mother may need a wrenching or a relieving experience, perhaps having perceived life with indifference, or still harboring grief over a related experience.

Incoming souls given up by the mother have experienced a cut-off from one of the most important ties a person can have. In another incarnation they may not have appreciated the bond of motherhood, or may have abused it, rejected it, or simply under-appreciated it, or may have been a child who left or hurt his parents. Having done the rejecting in another life they now have to experience rejection to fully understand that this is not God's plan.

On the other hand, the adoptive mother in this incarnation is des-perately seeking maternal satisfaction. Having not succeeded at natural conception, possibly due to having failed to appreciate the blessings of motherhood, she is now given the opportunity of having a child.

For instance, take the case of Jenny. In a channeled session Jenny was told the following by my spirit teachers:

> You have always had a burning desire to know God, Jenny, but you have had the confusion of not accepting where your respon-sibilities lie.
>
> When you lived in India, you were the mother of three chil-dren and the wife of a loving businessman. The first time you saw the Holy Man known as Hare Krishna you were standing by the side of the road. When your eyes locked with his, you were overcome with a desire to follow him. Despite your domestic obligations you abandoned your family to become one of his followers. Pleas from your children meant less than your desire to learn from this man. When Krishna spoke to you, telling you not to abandon your responsibility, you still left your family in order to follow this man.

When a surrogate mother refuses to let go of her child sometimes her soul memory is jogged, and while it is true that she is reneging on the promise of a contractual arrangement, sometimes nature can't be ignored. As in the case of infertility, nature has to be dealt with honestly. The Universal plan may be that the natural child stays with the natural mother. God may not care about contracts where a baby is concerned.

The mother's soul memory, or the Akashic record, may be touched when she's seeing her child for the first time, or it kicks in her womb and she realizes it belongs to her. Many of the fathers involved in the surrogate relationship have felt cheated, and have fought to the death to get their children, who often have come from their seed. Such a father may also have in his soul memory the experience of rejecting of an incoming child, or in some way failing to appreciate the bond of fatherhood.

Birth, Conception, and Families: Life Lessons

Hatred for, or lack of identity with, one's parents: often the result of a soul memory which cannot be obliterated.
LESSON: forgiveness, learning to love one another

Abortion, as an incoming fetus: soul needs the experience of rejection
LESSON: flexibility

Abortion, as a parent: comes from lack of faith, fear, or selfishness
LESSON: trust in God's plan, selflessness, and discernment

Miscarriage, Stillbirth: no soul to take the physical body
LESSON FOR PARENTS: faith in knowing there is a universal reason for everything, and all will be taken care of in God's time

Crib Death: as in miscarriage, incoming soul pulls out of the physical
LESSON FOR PARENTS: faith, there is a reason for everything

Infertility: possible lack of respect for life, need for education, or improper timing for incoming soul(s)

LESSON: reverence towards the Creator and all things Divine, "There is a time for everything under heaven."

Adoption, for the child: the soul needs experience of not having "roots"
LESSON: adjustment, appreciation, forgiveness, to overcome feelings of rejection by loving and receiving love

Adoption, for the birth parents: the soul needs the experience of loving another as if it were its own, moving toward universal love
LESSON: overcome ego, love unconditionally

Fertile Abundance: parents offer important experience for souls who are eager to incarnate
LESSON: trust, discernment, selflessness, and faith

Multiple birth siblings: the soul needs the experience of humility, of not being the only one
LESSON: sharing, developing identity, selflessness

We create the world we perceive.—Mark Engel

CHAPTER 14

How We Are Perceived

I wish I could say that I was born with a veil or that I underwent some other impressive mystical event during my formative years. In truth I was a shy, gawky, unattractive, sometimes neglected, child. But I was inquisitive; I like to think, intelligent, and passionately determined to help people help themselves even then.

In school my friends were equally gawky and unattractive, the "undesirables." But what a person was didn't affect me. What bothered me was their dissatisfaction with themselves, which often bordered on hopelessness, and their anger at others for making them uncomfortable. What baseless emotions these are. Even then I knew you could not heap responsibility upon others.

"If you are unhappy being fat, then stop eating spaghetti," I suggested at the lunch table. "If you have no friends, then be extra friendly."

What is the point in relaying this? To reinforce the idea that although there are karmic reasons for many of our situations, these are in place to initiate a growth experience. Remember Edgar Cayce's concept of transformation? Transformation is karma bringing on an adjustment in temperament so that the karma can then be withdrawn. As Cayce explains in reading 262-7,

Q. Explain what is meant by the transformation taking place or to take place in connection with the work of Edgar Cayce?
A. In an explanation, let's all understand in their own speech. To some, an awakening to the greater channels of power; to others, more spirituality than materiality. To others, the karmic influ-

ences have reached their changing point, that the vibrations may be brought one to another. In transformation comes a light for those that look for same.

Merely as an observer of natural phenomena, I am fascinated by my own personal appearance. This does not mean that I am pleased with it, mind you, or that I can even tolerate it. I simply have a morbid interest in it.—Robert Benchley , *My Face*

In reading 949-2, involving a man crippled by polio, Cayce said, "The body was *broken* through those experiences necessary . . . for the awakening of the inner man." In his former life, the man had jeered at others who had held to their ideals while being persecuted, so now his own handicap caused him to be highly sensitized to those with problems. Apparently he learned .that what you condemn in another, you become yourself.

Once the transformation was brought about the man no longer cursed his disease. He was able to understand it and work with it, and became successful in life and business. But a limp remained, perhaps as a reminder.

While it is understood that appearance and personality are largely influenced by heredity, very often there is an underlying karmic cause. People who have had lifetimes emphasizing a particular proficiency may find that skill or talent reflected again in their current physical make-up, as part of a pattern. Those who relied too heavily on one aspect of their being may now find it missing. Those previously lacking a certain quality may be presented with that particular physical feature to facilitate the adoption of the needed quality now.

The image of myself which I try to create in my own mind in order that I might love myself is very different from the image which I try to create in the minds of others in order that they may love me.—W. H. Auden

When Gerald appeared for his reading it was immediately apparent from his physique as well as his aura that he took part in a tremendous amount of athletic activity. Much of the information coming through for him involved past-life activities in this direction.

After his reading I listened to the tape. I generally have no conscious memory of the readings since they are channeled on a deeply subconscious basis. I heard my voice tell this young man, about whom I knew nothing other than a name and birthdate:

> In the golden age of Greece you were a Spartan athlete. You devoted your entire incarnation to the winning of sporting events and were in prime physical condition. You usually achieved the number one position of any event attempted.

This was followed by information about other lives where Gerald excelled in physical endeavors. Through it all I had the impression of being afloat, on water.

I asked him, "Are you a physical trainer or an athlete?"

He laughed and replied, "A personal trainer. But I want to compete as a swimmer in the Olympics."

"I believe you will compete in the Olympics. But I see that you need to work with other people first, to share and not be so exclusively competitive. Perhaps teaching swimming?"

He agreed that he had been contemplating coaching the high school swim team. Now it would be next on his agenda.

Sometimes, our physical beings reflect the pursuits of previous lifetimes. At other times, it is the result.

> The habit of looking for beauty in everything makes us notice the shortcomings of things; our sense, hungry for complete satisfaction, misses the perfection it demands.—George Santayana, *The Sense of Beauty*

Physical Shortcomings

Regarding the issue of physical beauty, I'd like to reiterate the saying that beauty is in the eye of the beholder. Of course we know this—that it is how we think of ourselves, and how we present ourselves, that we are perceived by others. Gerald thought of himself as an athlete, a fact easily picked up on visually or by anyone tuning into his aura, or thought waves. If we think of ourselves as ugly, sloppy, lazy, unlovable, that is how others perceive us.

That said, if we have difficulty presenting the image of confident attractiveness, if we fall into any extreme—such as projecting overt sexuality, or having a marked physical shortcoming—there is usually an underlying spiritual cause. Although every situation worked through gives us greater appreciation and balance, it is the *extremes* which I point out as having a definite karmic basis, not the minor issues that one's nose is too long or one's hair is not curly enough.

> Whenever we pretend, on all occasions, a mighty contempt for anything, it is a pretty clear sign that we feel ourselves very nearly on a level with it.—William Hazlittm, *On Vulgarity and Affectation*

So then why do some individuals look like supermodels, while others resemble the bearded lady at the circus? People who have not nourished their bodies, have previously misused them or let them atrophy, will not be blessed in a subsequent life with robust good looks. They will have to undergo a situation that engenders an appreciation of the work which goes into the upkeep of their physical temples.

Perhaps they will struggle to look appealing or perhaps they will become a fixture at the plastic surgeon's office, or perhaps they will accept their limitations and work on their inner selves. Whatever the situation, it presents a chance for change, for growth, and for appreciation.

Those people who have respected their bodies without vanity and without undue importance placed on this aspect of their beings are most likely to receive the blessing of physical beauty in future incarnations.

Obesity

Many of us struggle endlessly with obesity. Through a life reading for Ann we were able to understand her individual struggle with weight and why she could not get it off.

> Ann, you have had a lifetime in China, the most recent life before this incarnation. A female, the youngest among nine children, you were born into hardship and poverty. This life was a struggle for you simply to stay alive, a struggle which you eventually lost. You starved to death in a rice field before the age of thirty.

For Ann that was not all. The lifetime before that was in India, another existence of deprivation. If Ann had one small meal a day in that incarnation, she was lucky.

It is easy to understand how one life of starvation after another would result in obesity. From the moment of her birth, Ann had the feeling of wanting food. This intensified over her lifespan, resulting in such a need for satiation that even as she completed one meal she had the overwhelming desire to begin another.

> I'm keeping myself really fit, I tell myself. I pig out one week and starve the next. But the truth is I have gained and lost the same ten pounds so many times over and over again my cellulite must have deja-vu.—Lily Tomlin, *Search for Intelligent Life in the Universe*

Once realizing that the pattern had played out its time—in Ann's case the pattern of food deprivation—she relearned the process of functioning normally. With obesity, this often means separating emotional needs from genuine hunger.

As she came to accept the idea of food as physical sustenance, Ann put the knowledge into practice. She began to eat small healthy meals and learned to recognize when her hunger was satisfied. Soon eating was no longer combined with the long-ago ingrained feelings of fear and deprivation.

Did Ann lose the weight? Most of it—100 pounds came off the first year, with more to follow. She has not regained weight and feels her recovery is permanent.

Why can some people, on the other hand, eat voraciously and not gain a pound? Alan lived out a series of three religious incarnations. While all were short, they were enough to set a karmic pattern.

More important than the urges of planetary influences were the

drives, talent, and abilities which came to men in previous lives
on Earth.—Gina Cerminara,, *Many Mansions: The Edgar Cayce
Story on Reincarnation*

In Alan's first religious lifetime, he was a priest in a rural Mexican
village. His life was deliberately austere, devoid of physical trappings,
and by his own choice he ate very little.

In a subsequent incarnation, Alan was an ascetic who wore rags and
fasted often; again, eating little or nothing.

More recently Alan was a Tibetan monk. He had food available to
him, but chose instead to undergo rigorous religious training. He had
considered food insignificant, needed simply for sustenance.

Now, born into this life, Alan has married an American woman who
loves to cook. He eats to please her—in fact he enjoys the sumptuous
meals she encourages him to consume, but hardly gains an ounce.

A reward for past moderation? A pleasant balancing of lives spent in
willful deprivation? Probably both. And along with it, an understanding
that food can be appreciated and not abused.

Sometimes we use weight as a balm for past hurts, as insulation, or
a buffer of protection from some known or unknown threat. Often this
fear centers on the opposite sex, or on getting too close to other people.
Some of us are afraid of the attention we get—or may not get—when we
are at ideal weight. Others are afraid they are unworthy of real love,
and so keep the weight on so that they will truly be "unlovable."

Betty agreed when I told her that she had to deal with too many
come-ons from men when she was at her former weight. The emotional
groping she was avoiding now extended to include the physical desires
of even her own husband.

"I don't want sex with him, he is unappealing to me physically, I
think even repulsive."

As she sat, crying and unhappy, I understood the basis of her fear. I
was being given the impression of a former life in which she was made
to satisfy the needs of a demanding and brutish spouse.

Ann was paying a huge physical price for her fear. She had buffered
herself with weight, and had in fact married someone with a similar weight
problem though she was repulsed by obesity. She had to recognize this,
and get her husband to understand it as well so that they could move on.

While this was a past-life experience, it could have easily been a result of childhood abuse, physical or emotional. But being made to live through this experience is perhaps a message that people need to accept themselves no matter what others do, or don't do, to them.

So many factors of our existence have an emotional basis as the result of prior experiences. Appearance, manner, health, our relationships—all have a spiritual root cause which should be explored and removed, so that in this incarnation as Cayce says, " No longer is the entity then under the law of cause and effect, or karma, but rather in grace it may go on to the higher calling . . . (2800-2)

> Do I love you because you're beautiful, or are you beautiful because I love you?—Asked by the prince in Rodgers and Hammerstein's *Cinderella*

Demeanor

Personality traits can be broken down into root causes attributed to karmic lessons. Of these, fear plays a particular part.

Fear is mankind's greatest enemy, bringing in its wake doubt, uncertainty, and apprehension. It manifests itself in a myriad of known and unknown ways, including phobias, lack of confidence, over-confidence, neuroses, irritability, vanity, hatred, envy, selfishness, lack of faith, greed, intolerance, low aspiration—and on and on.

Fear must be exposed and dealt with, as brutally as possible.

William came for a reading out of desperation, and was frankly honest. His coworkers, his job superiors, and even his family had been complaining for years about his unbearable arrogance, he explained. Now his wife was leaving him.

Could such a personality defect be addressed and changed? It became immediately apparent why William had such a superior attitude. He had been a matador in Spain (explained my reading for him), adored, even worshiped because of his prowess in the ring as well as out of it. It seemed he had been a particular favorite of rich Senoras.

William had also lived as a celebrated Kabuki actor in seventeenth-century Japan.

"William, it is all well to be respected, loved, and revered. But since it is causing you such great pain to continue to expect this adoration, your need for it must be examined."

You see, William had been stabbed to death by a jealous husband in Spain, and in Japan he was unseated as one of the leading actors of his time by his own protégé. His current arrogance was born of fear.

"William, what are you afraid of?" I asked.

Practically everything, it seemed. Of being outdone at work, of being thought of as less than perfect. Fear of his wife not loving him. His fear had become a prophecy about to be fulfilled.

"William, take hold of yourself. Recognize that what happened in previous lifetimes is over and done with, and you can now go on with the business of being just William. Give your subconscious the message that arrogance is no longer part of your life. It is to be replaced by humility and modesty. Tell yourself this over and over. Believe it, and it will happen."

William believed it. He told his wife he loved her more than even himself, and he apologized to his coworkers. Was William presented with arrogance as a hurdle to overcome, in order to learn acceptance of his imperfect self and humility? I believe so. Once he recognized this, he proceeded with the process of healing.

> A man, to be greatly good, must imagine intensely and comprehensively; he must put himself in the place of another and of many others; the pains and pleasures of his species must become his own.—Shelley, *A Defence of Poetry*

Self-Importance

People who laugh at the concept of past lives usually say something like, "Oh, yeah, I was Cleopatra, just like everyone else. And next time I'll probably be a stone."

I would like to answer these individuals with, "Wrong, it is this time that you are a stone." But instead of doing that, I'll use an illustration.

In my experience, very few people who hear about their past lives learn that they were anyone famous. When regressed, the information usually confirms that we have been serfs, maids, soldiers, housewives, assistants, or partakers of equally mundane existences—with a few exceptions.

Jane couldn't believe that it was her ego which was causing her to experience the break-up of one relationship after another.

"But he was selfish," she pointed out. "And the one before that was a jerk. Just couldn't allow himself to experience love. Before that? He was a Momma's boy. Didn't want to move out of the house. Why do you ask?"

The truth was, men found her difficult, spoiled, egotistical, and generally, a big pain. I could read it in her aura and in her past lives. It was painfully obvious.

Under hypnosis, the full breadth of Jane's personality problem came out.

"Why, I am the queen of the world!" she proclaimed. "Why are you not kneeling? I will have you killed if you do not kneel!" Then she went on with a litany of why she was such a great ruler.

Each time Jane regressed it was more of the same. She was powerful, omnipotent; I was a peon who deserved to be thrown into prison.

After three sessions I had her listen to the tapes. She was shocked and amused, if not a trifle impressed. But she did admit that this was egotism and insensitivity at its worst. She went to work on that part of her nature, and she was so strong and determined that I truly believe she was successful.

I think that this one really may have been Cleopatra.

How We Are Perceived: Life Lessons

Shy, Gawky, Unattractive: Soul was beaten down in the past, perhaps as a slave; now needs to move beyond survival mode.
LESSON: Stand tall, breathe deeply, adopt courage and an aura of success, walking the road as a free and confident being.

Physical Shortcomings or Handicaps: Often a balancing for having used powers to intimidate and control others; or excessive ego without regard to consequences to others.
LESSON: Balance. Develop your spiritual potential. Respect others and they will respect you and bolster your self-esteem to the point where,

with effort, you will accomplish marvelous things.

Obesity or Other Weight Issues: Often the result of a lifetime of deprivation or starvation.
LESSON: Know that you have all that you need now, and that the Universal Creator will provide.

Self-Importance: Often a carry-over from a previous life in which you were royalty, or in a position of power over others.
LESSON: Take interest in others. Ask them about themselves, their work, their interests. Remember we are all equally children of God in our immortal soul state.

Fear of Putting Yourself out There: For too many years you were cut off and left to fend for yourself by others.
LESSON: Go out for a walk and breathe the fresh air deeply. Smile at everyone you pass and be amazed at the smiles you get back. Show enthusiasm and sociability for all and receive the same back. You might change the life of someone who was just like you.

> Character cannot be developed in ease and quiet. Only through experience of trial and suffering can the soul be strengthened, vision cleared, ambition inspired, and success achieved.
> —Helen Keller

> Love has been described as the harmony of two souls and the contact of two epidermes. It is also, from our infancy, the starting point of human relationships and needs.—*The Joy of Sex*, edited by Alex Comfort

CHAPTER 15

Love, Sex, and Relationships

Soul Mates

What is a soul mate? We hear the term thrown about, but does anyone really know what it means?

I define soul mate as a spiritual, emotional, and physical partner, with whom you can harmonize with in a learning and fulfilling way. More so, a soul mate can be a *lovemate*, a partner who complements your weaknesses and fleshes out your strengths. A soul mate is not only someone with whom you may have had shared experience with in former incarnations, but who grows with you as you work out things in this lifetime together.

A soul mate is our cosmic counterpart. A soul mate is the highest expression of our soul's purpose because a relationship with this individual forces us to function in an unselfish, benevolent, caring, considerate way. The merging of the consciousness of soul mates can generate creativity, a feeling of euphoria, and sexual harmony leading to ecstasy. Yet these relationships can also be completely celibate. Sisters, brothers, and neighbors can be soul mates. Soul mate relationships don't have to be romantic; it can be a connection that does not involve commitment and there can be more than one in your life. Your soul mate is a person who feels like your missing half whether you're with him or her, or away from each other. The relationship can be euphoric when the two of you are working in harmony, or it can be volatile and unfulfilling when the soul's growth is not equal on the part of both people.

When there is growth in soul-mate relationships, the relationships sometimes end when the responsibilities, projects, or involvements that brought the two together have ended. Permanence is not necessarily a part of soul mate relationships. Yet partnerships involving unfinished karma are probably the strongest relationships of all.

Unhealthy Relationships

There is no such thing as a "wrong" relationship. There are difficult relationships, unhealthy relationships, even abusive relationships, but every relationship is in its own way, karmically productive. Even the worst, most tragic of situations is a working through of past karma, intended to bring about balance and understanding on the part of the soul. It is when the soul fails to recognize and learn from the unhealthiness, that a relationship becomes bad.

All relationships are karmic on some level. When there is unfinished business between souls between incarnations, marriage is one of the most effective, if not intensive, ways of working it out. This is not to say there aren't easy relationships; two past unhappy lovers may be uniting; two formerly unloving mates may be now loving and relating to each other, or maybe the two parties are just so concordant with one another that they have to be together again. But when everyone is telling a particular individual that her relationship is bad, that her partner is wrong for her—even diabolic—you can be sure that it is a karmic relationship.

If an individual in a relationship is needy, squeamishly so, it maybe correction for a time before, when her partner was the one who was overly needy, even handicapped to the point of having her perform all his tasks for him. Now it is her turn. If a mate is violent or wickedly jealous, maybe his partner inflicted cruelty on his person last time around. Maybe she gave him legitimate cause to be jealous, and this is now her chance to act out of fullness and love, assuring him and strengthening his ability to trust. Whatever the situation is, be sure that both parties need to work it through together, so that together they can learn the process of love and forgiveness. But do not mistake relationship karma for ingrained patterns which have to be overcome.

Sometimes everyone around a certain individual has grasped the message of negativity in his relationships, except the person in question. Until he has accepted the futility and destructiveness of his own patterns, on his own, there is nothing anyone can do except remind him that he is good, and worthy of giving, as well as receiving, genuine love.

> There is no sexual relationship which doesn't involve responsibility, because there are two or more people involved: anything which militantly excludes a partner is hurtful, yet to be whole people we have at some point to avoid total fusion with each other—"I am I and you are you, and neither of us is on earth to live up to the other's expectations." People who communicate sexually have to find their own fidelities.—*The Joy of Sex*, edited by Alex Comfort

When the individual has grasped that the experience is no longer necessary, he can empower himself to change, for he no longer needs it as part of the current incarnation.

So, there is no such thing as a wrong partner, and no such thing as a mistake. Realize that a person is not right in the long run, because he causes you pain, then move through it and out of it. Recognize, grow, and learn. It's as simple as that.

We all have choices, decisions, and free will, and we can either continue in an experience that is detrimental to our soul's development, or move up and out of it to beneficial and fulfilling experiences. The key is to acknowledge a situation for what it is, and either improve it, or move on.

Non-Existent Relationships

People who can't seem to find healthy, balanced relationships are often unable to accept that they deserve such a thing as love and the fulfillment which comes with this, or just too disillusioned to believe that the possibility exists. The fact is that everything we need as human beings is available to us here on Earth. It is up to us to obtain it. See it, breathe it, and believe it—in every cell of your being.

> Romance novels are read by more than 50 million American women. They account for 46% of mass-market paperback sales and create a $1 billion industry each year (Associated Press,

1996). Every month 120 new titles are published and most sell
out.——Rhoda Unger, Mary Crawford, *Women and Gender*

Recognize and destroy negative roadblocks such as believing yourself too old, unattractive, or unlovable. Recognize and acknowledge that
there are other, less worthy people finding love and happiness right
this very minute.

Think of the hypnotist in his nightclub act who makes a man believe
he is in a small box. Try as he may, the man is unable to climb out, for
his mind believes and accepts his limitations— until the hypnotist tells
him otherwise.

We repeat patterns, negative or positive, from lifetime to lifetime
until something happens to make us alter that pattern. Sometimes the
pattern ends because we become tired and discouraged with ourselves.
When this happens it seems as if we are reborn.

When Lucy came for a consultation she was just short of completing
her second divorce. Her spouses had proven abusive and dependent
on alcohol or drugs. The men she dated in-between were equally dysfunctional. I suggested a hypnotic regression, the quickest way to the
root of the problem.

Regressed to the early years of childhood, Lucy relived scorn and
debasement doled out by her father.

"What a brat you are, Lucy," eventually became, "No one could ever
love you."

Under hypnosis a previous lifetime was revealed wherein Lucy was a
male in Sardinia who was abusive toward the women in his life. Women
to Lucy in that incarnation were belongings to be discarded or used at
discretion, and as a male she did this without reservation.

Lucy was amazed by the tape, yet it made great sense to her. She
had been programmed right from the start to think nothing of herself,
and to expect nothing—which is exactly what she got. As she probed
her problem, it melted from her. I could see understanding and respect
in the tilt of her head as she began to accept what everyone else knew
right along—that she was entitled to happy relationships.

Sometimes, we can change our standards by discerning why our
self-esteem is so low, and then do whatever is necessary to raise it.

In *Love and Addiction*, Stanton Peele and Archie Brodsky give criteria for separating love from "addiction:"

1.   Does each partner have a secure belief in his or her own value?

2.   Are they improved by the relationship, are they better, stronger more attractive, more accomplished, or more sensitive individuals? Do they value the relationship for this very reason?

3.   Do partners maintain serious interests outside the relationship, including other meaningful personal relationships?

4.   Is the relationship integrated into, rather than set apart from, the totality of the partners' lives?

5.   Are the partners beyond being possessive or jealous of each other's growth and expansion of interest?

6.   Are the partners also friends? Would they seek each other out if they should cease to be primary partners?

Infidelity

Ron found it impossible to stay faithful to one woman. He explained this to me with a self-effacing smile. It wasn't that he didn't want to be in a monogamous relationship, he just didn't know how to respond in a one-on-one, committed way. Besides, he found it impossible to resist the lure of having more than one woman at a time. But his ex-wife now hated him, and he barely ever saw his child.

Working with Ron was not easy since he was reluctant to give up womanizing. But he insisted that he wanted to change for the better, and I eventually saw that he truly did crave emotional stability and self-realization.

Regressed to the age of seven, Ron spoke brokenheartedly.

"Mommy, Mommy," he sobbed, "I will take care of you, I will, I will."

His dad was seeing other women, his adult self knew. The little boy self knew only that his mother was deeply hurt. Yet she returned again and again to the man who hurt her. Was this how men and women related?

We also discovered a lifetime of Ron's in Argentina, where he was known for his conquests of 'unattainable' women—virgins, wives, girls of royal birth, and so on. He was a true Don Juan. He never married and truly enjoyed being catered to by women throughout that entire incarnation. Why would he give up such treatment?

We went back to a more recent lifetime in Spain, where Ron tried to do much the same as he had done in Argentina. But whereas in Argentina he was hailed as a hero, in Spain he had become ruthless. Several women were ruined as a result of his indiscriminate boasting, and he embarked in blackmailing schemes to support his obsession. Worst of all, he acted with no remorse or regret.

Now the karmic "chickens were coming home to roost." Ron's life was being torn apart by his selfish treatment of women, much the same way that he had torn others' lives apart.

We are the product of our childhood and our past lives. Whether we are victims of these experiences or winners is very much our own doing. My hope is that Ron gave up his womanizing and returned to his family.

> How few are our real wants! And how easy is it to satisfy them!
> Our imaginary ones are boundless and insatiable.—Julius Chas.
> Hare and Augustus William Hare's *Guesses at Truth*

The bottom line is that people who follow a pattern of infidelity are driven by a deep inner desire to find their own highest nature and selves. When you know who you are, are at peace with your inner and outer self, and express an inner tranquility, the pattern of looking for yourself in the highest and lowest of experiences, will not occur.

Homosexuality

Although we incarnate in the earth as male or female, the soul was neither male nor female at the time of Creation. When in your incarnations you go too far in one direction, such as when you're male too many times and the soul becomes unbalanced, the switch occurs. As Edgar Cayce said, you cannot always be male or always female. When the soul expresses too much of one gender it's time to switch to balance the experience. A soul is not always happy about this, or ready for that changeover. Their consciousness may be all one way, and then all of a sudden they're in the opposite gender. It is not so easy to catch up. A previous man, who was perfectly happy as a male, now suddenly finds a big bow in his hair and wonders, what's that about? These souls are simply not ready for the gender change, and fight it all the way.

The physical body reflects that the soul is not ready, in that person's opinion. But while their personality is not ready, their highest God expression, that knows what's needed, is ready, and there's the conflict. Homosexuality is another instance of conflict, between personal desire and the highest soul's purpose.

Bob's reading showed that he had lived recently in France as a woman. He was adored by his nobleman husband, and died early from an illness without having borne any children. In fact, Bob had lived at least seven lives as a woman, we found.

Shortly after the incarnation in France, Bob was born as a male in America, in 1961. As a child he related not with his brothers and their aggressive games, but identified with his sister, although he tried not to show this to anyone. As he grew older, it was boys who attracted Bob's sexual interest, though again, he tried not to show this to anyone.

In college he had his first homosexual experience, which facilitated an entry into the homosexual lifestyle. Why is any of this of note, when in fact Bob's story could be one of a hundred, one of a thousand?

He was desperately unhappy, and wanted to know what was at the core of his 'differentness.'

We regressed Bob to the period of time spent in France. He indicated that at the time of his death he was anxious to be born into another physical body, although with trepidation about coming in as a male. He was given the option of staying in the world of spirit a while longer to readjust to the change-over to maleness. But he was intent on reincarnating.

In retrospect, Bob believed that maybe it had been too soon, and that he had not in fact made a full adjustment. This understanding was what Bob needed to accept his homosexuality.

I believe that men and women are homosexual for a variety of reasons. It can be for balance, or it can be a corrective experience, to enable the soul to accept those who may be "different" by becoming that way themselves.

**Sex is one of the nine reasons for reincarnation,
wrote novelist Henry Miller.
The other eight are unimportant.**

Divorce and Long-Term Relationships

Most of us need more than one person to be in our life as a lover or a marital partner, simply because of the tremendous influx of souls as we begin this new age. In our lifetime we've advanced from the Iron Age to the space age to cyber space; from linear to multi-dimensional thinking; from a population of one-half billion people to more than six billion souls on the earth. As such, there are many new challenges and varieties of experience in this age, providing unique and tremendous opportunity for soul growth.

Because of this acceleration of karmic experience, there may be the need to finish up karmic interaction with a number of people before the patterns can be completed and everyone can move on. Ideally this karmic interaction can be completed in loving relationships that will end amicably without divorce, but often this is not the case.

On the other hand, long-term marriages and relationships are possible, when the souls postpone the working out of other relationships for another time, and choose instead to grow together and deal with the challenge of long-term interaction.

> An understanding of Harlequin romances should lead one less to condemn the novels than the conditions which have made them necessary. Even though the novels can be said to intensify female tensions and conflicts, on balance the contradictions in women's lives are more responsible for the existence of Harlequins than Harlequins are for the contradictions.—Tania Modleski, *Loving with a Vengeance: Mass Produced Fantasies for Women*

Sex

Ascetics maintain that physicality is a substitute for nirvana; that once the Godhead is achieved, sex will seem like the cast-off of a poor man. But few of us have yet reached the Godhead state of oneness with the Creator, and fewer still are ready to cast off our sexuality. I believe that happy, fulfilled sexuality is given to us in the meantime as a gift.

Sex at its best between two loving partners is in itself a cosmic experience, an attunement. Until we reach the stage of full enlightenment, enjoyment of sex is our right as human beings.

Lack of sex, or lack of enjoyment of having sex, is sometimes the continuation of a past-life choice for celibacy, without the current personality realizing it. Unfulfilling sex may be the outcome of repressed fears and anxieties. Or it may be the result of childhood influence, or a pattern of repression or abuse set by others that has to be overcome. First, go back to the root of the problem before trying to restructure sexual interest and expression.

Over-reliance on sex on the other hand, is often the trait of powerful or controlling people who rely too heavily on the physical in order to maintain the level of drive and power to which they aspire. It may be a substitute for control, or a tool used to exert control. Often this over-reliance is the result of lives spent in dominant positions, where sex was a function, rather than an expression of feelings or togetherness.

Sexual manipulation, putting a price on sexuality, or any subtle form of sexual barter is often a holdover of pay for sex, a pattern from previous incarnations where there was a return for sexual favors—gifts, instead of normal give-and-take.

Extreme cases of sexual anesthesia, the result of physical issues—surgery, an accident, prescription drugs—may also have an underlying karmic cause. It can be a current response to a former sexual trauma such as rape or physical debasement in this lifetime or one previous. It could be due to a fear, such as fear of pregnancy, or the result of severe misuse of sexuality.

Whatever the cause, sexual anesthesia is a severing from the physical, a total shutdown of all things sexual. While you may be performing the motions, there is no sensation and no enjoyment. Sexual healing for this is sustained fidelity and caring by you and by your partner, commitment, and heightened awareness of each other's needs.

Sex is a decision.—Ellen Kreidman

Love, Sex and Relationships: Life Lessons

Inability to give or receive love: Love is the most powerful spiritual force in the universe, expressing the greatest qualities of the soul. True love, which comes from the Creator, is untainted by jealousy, possessiveness, lack of trust, or selfishness. These issues are often caused by repeat disappointments in love, or growing up in an environment with little loving expression.

LESSON: Practice what the Master said: "Love one another as I have loved you."

Loyalty, fidelity, monogamy: These show that you are at the end of a long cycle of relationship challenges.

LESSON: You are reaping the rewards of what you have sown.

Infidelity, immaturity in relationships, inability to commit: The pattern you have set up for yourself is destructive to yourself and others.

LESSON: Your soul needs the lesson of trust. Believe that the person you are with is the one you are meant to be with at this point in time.

Sexual dysfunction: Everything from premature ejaculation to impotence may have root cause in past lives.

LESSON: Patience, effort, and forbearance are what is needed.

Inflicting spousal abuse: Continuation of negative patterns, possession by evil influences, need for self-justification and control.

LESSON: Harm, inflicted especially on those weaker than yourself, will be returned to you tenfold. Learn selfless love and respect for others, as well as yourself.

Accepting Spousal Abuse: The need for punishment is a result of a negative pattern.

LESSON: Learn that allowing others to do harm is not a form of love. Learn self-worth.

Overt Kinkiness/Promiscuity: Fear and hurt stemming from cravings out of control.

LESSON: Learn self-worth and self-love.

Part IV

In Practice

CHAPTER 16

Case Studies

Love, Sex, and Relationships

THE PROBLEM: *Difficulty Finding Soul Mate*

Joan was an attractive woman, about thirty-five years of age. Not overweight or underweight, she was well-groomed, intelligent, well-spoken and nicely dressed.

"Joyce, I'm ready to give up. I've tried expensive dating services, run personal ads, enlisted the help of friends, and have just about run out of ideas. I'm starting to think that I'll never find that right person . . . my biological clock is ticking! I will never find someone to love me, much less my soul mate!"

I asked if she had ever been hypnotized.

Laughing, she answered, "I'll bet that I would be very hard to hypnotize. I find it difficult to relax."

I told her not to worry. All she had to do was close her eyes and listen to the sound of my voice. She would remain in control of her body, mind, and spirit. I would just be a guide and a friend.

She looked at me for a moment, and then enthusiastically said, "Let's do it!"

THE KARMIC REASON: *Inability to Commit*

Joan proved to be an excellent subject. When she was in a light state of hypnosis, she started speaking softly.

I said, "Joan, where are you?"

"I'm not sure . . . it's very cold . . . "

"Do you see a newspaper?"

"Yes . . . "

"I can't hear you . . . please speak up."

"Yes."

"What is the date or year on the newspaper?"

"December, 1917 . . . I am a soldier . . . we are going to war . . . I am an eighteen–year–old man . . . I am saying good–bye to a young girl. She is kissing me and crying."

"Move five years forward . . . "

"I am living on a farm . . . there are a number of young women around me . . . all seem eager to love me . . . I am not interested in any of them."

"Move ten years forward. What do you see?"

"Three young women. One is holding a baby. She tells me it is mine. She's crying now . . . asks me if I will marry her . . . I refuse. . . . I tell her that I cannot be with just one woman . . . I am walking away from these women . . . "

"Did you ever settle down or marry in that lifetime?"

"No . . . I am alone . . . "

THE SOLUTION:

After I brought Joan out of her regression, I received the following message for her and for others who are looking for that "special some-one":

Know in your heart, mind, and spirit that you have learned the lessons from the past. Learn to recognize love when it presents itself. Know that freedom of the spirit does not have to be confined by a love relationship. Believe that the joy and enrichment of being in a love relationship can allow the spirit to soar. Allow love to replace fear.

Healing affirmation:

This affirmation should be written on a white 3x5 card, and carried with you. It should be repeated throughout the day. "My heart, mind, and spirit are open, and ready to receive the love that I desire, and richly deserve."

Further Suggestions:

Carry a pink quartz crystal close to your heart. Consider using the aromatherapy oils or scents, "Champaca," or "ylang–ylang," in a diffuser or bath soak.

FINAL OUTCOME

When I last spoke with Joan, she was dating two men, one named Michael, and the other Jim. She was very fond of both men, and having trouble deciding who would make the best mate. She was enjoying the experience.

THE PROBLEM: *Sexual Frigidity*

Dana is a very attractive thirty–year–old. She had been dating Tim for five years. Even though she seems to fall within the parameters of what we would label as "beautiful" and "sexually appealing," she says she is completely disinterested in sex, having never had a satisfying sexual experience.

"Can you believe that I've never had a sexually fulfilling relationship or experience? I would love to experience prolonged sensuality and mind–blowing sex! Why is it that all of my sexual encounters leave me feeling frustrated? Is it me?" She continued, "Why don't any men know how to bring me sexual satisfaction?"

Getting Dana to relax, and to let go of tension, was not easy. Eventually, though, we were successful, and she could be regressed.

When deeply relaxed, Dana began speaking, first inaudibly and then clearly. "Could it be . . . I think I'm a prostitute . . . I am in Napoleon's court . . . no, I'm not a prostitute, I'm a courtesan!"

"What is the year?"

"The year . . . it feels like it's around . . . 1805 . . . "

"Are you happy in this lifetime?"

"Happy . . . no! I have no life . . . I belong to the court . . . I hate Napoleon and his men . . . they are filthy and foul-smelling . . . I swear to myself that I will never have sex again . . . "

"Do you have any joy in this life?"

"No . . . (crying softly) . . . as a matter of fact . . . I am thrown into jail and left to rot . . . it is dark, and there is no food or water . . . "

THE KARMIC REASON: *Physical and Emotional Overload and Saturation*

Bringing her to a semi–awake level, where she was very open to suggestion, I said, "Dana, this will never happen to you again . . . there is no reason for you to be sad. You are in America, and have every reason to be happy and fulfilled. The lifetime or lifetimes of sexual overload or saturation have caused you to experience spiritual fatigue and disinterest. You no longer have a reason to be physically detached from your sensuality."

The Solution:

Understand that this is a whole new lifetime, and that you are in a new physical body. You have every right to experience sensual pleasure. This time around, you are in control of your body and your experiences.

Know that healing of the spirit can take place when understanding brings enlightenment and renewal.

Healing Affirmation:

"I am not a victim of any situation. I have earned the gift of spiritual regeneration and renewal."

Other Suggestions:

Introduce or acquaint yourself with your own sensuality. Enjoy full–body massages; use body oils. Try aromatherapy, particularly "Geranium Rose."

FINAL OUTCOME

When I last saw Dana she was smiling. It was the smile of a happy woman.

CHAPTER 17

Questions and Answers

The following are my personal answers to the recurring questions I've been asked on my television and radio shows, and in private sessions. They are based on my studies, experiences, knowledge, beliefs, and readings I have given.

QUESTION: Is there meaning to life?

Yes! Absolutely. One-hundred percent! That is "moksha," and explained in the Introduction.

QUESTION: Does God really exist?

The answer has to be, yes . . . why? Because He created us . . . do any of us have the slightest idea about how to make us? Hair? Skin? Nails . . . and all that we are?

QUESTION: Are my prayers heard? If so, why aren't they answered?

Prayers are heard and acknowledged within the keeping of your karmic soul record. Occasionally, there is "special" or "divine intervention," so that karma can be "tweaked" a little . . . in some cases, eliminated altogether.

QUESTION: Do we have free will?

Most people have approximately 12–15% free will, so that decisions can be made, and so that soul growth can occur. The rest, about 85–88%, is karma.

QUESTION: Is that the reason so few psychic readings are 100% accurate? Is it because it is so difficult to determine the way humans will use their free will?

Yes . . . absolutely. Psychic readings can be very helpful, and a great

light along the path of life, but only God is correct 100% of the time.
QUESTION: Can all psychics read the soul record?
Only psychics who are of high enough spiritual vibration, have access
to a person's soul or Akashic Record. Of course, those psychics are
the most accurate. They are not necessarily the most famous or most
sought-after psychics. Again, you have to use your discernment in
choosing and knowing those who are, "real" or valid, from the ones
who are not. Appearances do not count, when seeking a psychic who
can read your karmic record.
QUESTION: When we die, do we have to account for our actions on
the earth? If so, how is that done?
After physical death, the body is cast off, but the soul merges with the
non-physical world. There are many dimensions and planes. The soul
goes to the correct plane, with the assistance of angelic souls who have
the specific job of guiding souls to their correct position. It is all very
welcoming and comforting.
QUESTION: What happens after physical death?
There are cleansing and purifying energies that help the soul to move
out of the earth's energies, and on to higher dimensions. After a period
of rest and restoration, which can last in a split second of earth time,
or centuries, the soul has what is known as the, "panorama," or life
review. Not a thing is left out of this review, and there is no judgment.
The only judgment comes from one's self, in realizing how things could
have been—and possibly should have been—better, while on the earth.

When the soul is ready, there is a period of judgment, where karmic deeds and actions are evaluated by the Angels of Karma. The soul
record, or Akashic record, is taken into account at that time. Was the
soul's mission fulfilled? Were wounds healed between relatives, or new
ones created? Were the correct bonds between people formed? Were the
wrong ones ended? Was there greed instead of generosity? Was forgiveness given when it should have been? Were sacred trusts broken, and so
on . . . there are so many soul experiences, and so many responsibilities.
However, there should also be pleasure and enjoyment on the earth.

The earth is not meant to be just a "vale of tears." There should be
joy, or course, and there should be celebrations. The soul experience
on the earth must be layered, intriguing, and challenging. It's a great
school of learning.

The time after physical death is often called "Summerland," because each death experience brings with it summer vacation! When we "go home," it is restorative and regenerative from the time spent on Earth. We are greeted by our spirit-teachers, guides, and departed loved ones. Usually, the first faces who greet us are our departed moms, dads, grandparents, or siblings. It's a huge party, just as it is when there is a birth on the earth. There is no sadness or grief, after passing. There is no remorse, and no clinging to the physical body, or place of residence or employment. The only time that occurs is if the departed person refuses to leave their surroundings. There are always strong lights, music, and entities to greet the departing person. If they refuse to leave their earthly surroundings, they can and will stay for as long as they choose to do so. Eventually, though, that will become tiresome, and they will leave with their angels and guides.

QUESTION: What determines physical death?

Well, it certainly is not the taking of one's last breath, because we all know about near-death experiences (NDES)—people coming back to life, after being clinically dead for a number of minutes, or hours. .

Therefore, it has to be something of far greater importance than the last breath, or the temporary stopping of the heart or pulse. The answer is the breaking of the "silver cord," or as the Hindus call it, the *Sutratma*.

The silver cord is an invisible life-giving connection between humans and their oversoul, or God-essence. Once it is broken, there is no turning back, or reclaiming the body. It is the final stage of the earthly incarnation. Because it is invisible, it can only be seen with the third eye (spiritual vision), or by psychics who are able to perceive the true state of physical death.

QUESTION: Do animals have souls?

There are "group souls" with animals, so, "yes," they do have souls.

QUESTION: What are crib deaths?

The incoming soul has the first six months of life to decide whether they will stay in the body or leave; when the life situation is too easy, difficult, or not right for their soul's development or enrichment, they will choose to leave, hence, "a crib death."

QUESTION: What happens to someone like Hitler?

God loves all of His children. All souls have the opportunity of "correction." In other words, at the appropriate time, Hitler will be given the opportunity of balancing his actions, and correcting his earthly deeds. He may be given the chance, for example, to work as a healer in a Leprosy colony, or in a very difficult situation that would challenge him on many levels. He might have these challenging experiences until his karmic record is cleared, and his soul is balanced.

QUESTION: Do drugs and alcohol harm one's spiritual growth, or as with certain drugs, enhance the experience?

Drugs and alcohol cause a person's electrical field, or aura, to be open, dark, and torn, rather than protected, whole, and brilliant. When the aura is damaged, as from drugs, alcohol, or illness, the human psyche will also be abnormal or damaged.

This can also occur from not only drugs, alcohol, and illness, but from dishonesty, damage to others, and acts of perversion.

Healing of the physical body, mind or spirit, starts with healing the aura, or auric shield. Healers work first on healing and sealing the aura, and then on the physical body.

QUESTION: Are Ouija boards safe to use?

For most people who are not developed or experienced mediums, and who do not know how to properly shield, protect, and direct the spirit experience, the Ouija is an extremely dangerous tool to use, and not at all a game. It's really a mistake that it is considered a "game," when in fact it is an open door to both dark and light spirit energies. The Ouija connection sends out a beam of light, which essentially says, "Open door to spirit, anyone can come in who wishes to do so." It will be very difficult for your angelic forces to protect you. It is a spiritually haphazard adventure.

In addition, because it does recklessly open a spirit door, it can be very difficult to eliminate unwanted, evil, or wandering spirits.

QUESTION: What about séances, or spirit circles?

The answer is that it can be both good and bad. It depends upon the quality of the medium, and whether or not they are karmic lightwork-ers, or at worst, participants in dark activities. An experienced medium, who works only with God, in most cases will bring into the séance only forces of light or good energy. However, again there should be a big warning given with all involvements with spirit gatherings.

QUESTION: Is it okay to be involved in witchcraft?

In my opinion, any time there is a bending, or interfering with someone else's karma, there is always a big red stop sign! There should never be any kind of interference with anyone's destiny, whether it is through witchcraft, voodoo, Santeria, or any other type of interference. The only karmically acceptable practice is prayer, wherein a favor is being requested, along with a request for special intervention. Gratitude must always be expressed, and is the most important part of prayer.

QUESTION: What are handicaps? What are physical abnormalities?

They are usually nothing more than a soul correction, or a balancing of karma. It is nothing more than an experience and opportunity that is given to the handicapped person and all of the people who are involved.

QUESTION: Where do animals go when they die?

They usually stay with us in the non–physical state. However, they are also free to roam and to experience all that they wish, but usually only within the animal kingdom.

QUESTION: Do animals have karma?

No, they do not. They are on the earth to fulfill the expression of their duties, which often include love, and the edification of the human species.

QUESTION: Do animals have souls?

Animals have "group souls," where they belong to a specific group of animals who incarnate at similar times, with similar life experiences. They often look very similar, and can recognize each other. They often will mourn throughout a lifetime about the separation from their mother and siblings, or the death of a companion animal.

QUESTION: Why do so many people experience so much pain and suffering before their physical death?

The soul chooses to do so. It is much easier to work off, and correct karma, while still in the physical body, rather than after crossing over.

QUESTION: Do you think there will be an End of Days?

Absolutely not. The earth is an extremely valuable school for learning, unique and quite special. There have been many times when there could have been atomic attacks, or other conflagrations, that were mysteriously stopped in their initial stages, thanks to divine intervention.

QUESTION: Are we ever really alone?

The answer is simply, No! We have one guardian angel who is with us from the time prior to our physical birth, throughout every moment of our life, and through and after the death experience.

QUESTION: Are there other angels as well?

Yes . . . there are many . . . there are karmic recording angels, angels of protection, angels of communication, angels of healing, angels of prosperity, and angels for just about anything and everything you can think of . . . they are all happy to work with humans. In addition, they grow in spirit through service. God and His angels love human beings.

QUESTION: If there are angelic forces, why are there accidents?

There are no accidents. Accidents are learning experiences, or karmic adjustments. Angels step back and away, when an accident is supposed to occur.

QUESTION: Is it possible to sell one's soul to the devil, or to the dark side, for fame and fortune?

Absolutely! For example, it would be very difficult for some to succeed on a grand scale in the music industry, and in Hollywood, without making this agreement. The rewards are usually great, and the price is inordinately high.

QUESTION: What is the difference between a soul mate, split soul, and twin flame?

A soul mate is usually someone we have incarnated with a number of times, and with whom there is unfinished karma. A twin soul is similar to a soul mate, but usually in a more compatible, less challenging relationship. A split soul is a person who incarnates as more than one person, at the same time, on the earth . . . for example, twins, or multiple births. The reason behind split-soul incarnations is for the acceleration of karma.

QUESTION: What is grace?

Grace is divine intervention . . . when there is a karmic lesson that is eliminated or made easier, in response to fervent, heart-felt prayer and supplication.

QUESTION: What does it mean to be 'born again?'

It is a religious belief . . . the fact is that we are born, again and again, and that is all the "born-again" experience that most humans need to have. It doesn't seem to have much effect on one's karmic challenges.

QUESTION: Do we choose our parents, or what?

The answer is a resounding, "Yes!" Whether we think it's a good choice or not, the higher mind, or greater consciousness, knows best. The correct parents and children are always the correct karmic choice.

QUESTION: Why do some babies, children, teens, and young adults have brief or abbreviated lifetimes?

There very often is a combining of lifetimes. That means, for example, if a person committed suicide at the age of 30, they might return to Earth for another 30 or 40 years. It's a balancing act, meaning that there are other karmic repercussions as well, such as deliberately shortening another person's life, or ignoring someone who needed assistance in another lifetime.

Remember the words of Ralph Waldo Emerson, who said, "Fate is nothing but the deeds committed in a prior state of existence."

QUESTION: Why don't we remember past lives?

We may not consciously remember past lives, but every one of our thoughts, words, and deeds are indelibly etched in our soul record, which follows us from lifetime to lifetime. If we remembered past lives on a conscious level, we would be extremely confused, or even insane. A veil separates human memory on a conscious level, separating lifetimes. If this were not the case, one lifetime would run right into the other. There is a cosmic law that each lifetime has to stand clearly on its own, without previous lifetime memories or obvious interaction.

QUESTION: What is the ultimate purpose of reincarnation, or re-birth?

Soul perfection. Re-connection with God, or reuniting with the God-head in a state of bliss or perfection. It is what is known by Hindus as "Nirvana." As we grow in soul perfection and godliness, we eventually come to the point of being able to truly "sit at the right hand of God." At that point, of soul perfection, we return to what is known as "The Source."

QUESTION: Do we incarnate as both male and female?

Yes, absolutely. All humans must have the experience of incarnating as both male and female.

QUESTION: How does astrology relate to karma and reincarnation?"

The astrological birth chart, when read correctly, gives a perfectly clear picture of one's life path; their destiny, challenges, highs, lows, and just about everything else one needs to know . . . it is a life photo that is given before a person incarnates . . . it is a basic pattern of what may be expected of that individual. The key word here is, "basic," because we must remember that there is always "free will," and that will always be the determining ultimate decision-making factor. The astrological chart is just a basic road map . . . the actions that a person takes are what determine their karmic outcome. The astrological chart is a complete astrological blueprint, and is known as the "natal chart." It contains a wheel of twelve houses, which indicate planetary placements at the time and location of a person's birth. Think of this chart as your "personal sky." The planets (this includes the sun and moon) and their interpretation are:

THE SUN indicates the inner core of a person's character;

THE MOON indicates the soul and emotional makeup;

MERCURY indicates the process of the mind, and communication;

VENUS governs love, harmony, art, and the power of attraction;

MARS governs human drive, ambition, assertiveness, and sexuality;

JUPITER governs wisdom, good fortune, money, and expansion;

SATURN governs freedom through discipline, work, and duty;

URANUS governs originality, spontaneity, and ingenuity;

NEPTUNE governs fantasy, drugs, delusion, glamour, and the underworld; and

PLUTO governs soul growth and transformation, breaking psychological and emotional locks.

Each of the houses is governed by a planet, and indicates a different aspect of the individual. Taken together, the placement of the planets presents an amazingly clear "three-dimensional" portrait.

The placement of the aforementioned sun signs, in any particular house, has great karmic significance.

One of the problems that people have with general astrology is that it is based strictly on the sun sign, which may or may not be an adequate indication of their personality and life direction. We are the sum of all our parts. The sun sign though, can be a useful, quick depiction and an integral part of our entire makeup, and is in place for another reason. Each sun sign comes with a particular set of characteristics or the basic personality. This is an indication of the incoming soul's greatest needs.

Since the astrological Nodes are always in opposite signs, when your South Node is, for example, in the sign of Gemini, your North Node will be in the opposite sign of Sagittarius. Again, humans incarnate to use and express the energy of their North Node, and to overcome the lessons of their prior incarnation—the energy of the South Node.

QUESTION: What do we know about the soul?

We believe that the soul is immortal and everlasting. Energy cannot be created or destroyed.

QUESTION: Is the soul perfect?

The soul is perceived to be, and is, indeed, perfect. It is God's gift to us, and is completely and irrevocably connected to the Creator. One's personality, however, can be less than perfect, and is usually the cause of the creation of new karma.

QUESTION: What is love?

Love is the expression and opportunity that humans are given during

QUESTION: Who is our spiritual creator? Who or what is God?

God, or the Creator, or whatever you wish to call God, is the provider of perfect experience, or karma, for our soul's growth.

QUESTION: What is the angelic 'filter?'

The invisible filter is that through which karmic information comes from the highest or angelic realms, and is within each person's Akashic soul record.

QUESTION: What does "transcendence" mean?

"Transcendence" means the karmic memory and experience which goes with each person, both before and after each of their lifetimes.

QUESTION: What is the personality? Is it the same as the soul?

The personality and soul are different. The soul is your spiritual counterpart and companion. The personality is the expression of your greatest mission. Your personality is your guide to expressing your soul's expression and mission.

> Your personality is that part of you that was born into, lives within, and will die within time. To be a human and have a personality are the same thing. Your personality, like your body, is the vehicle of your evolution.—Gary Zukav, *Seat of the Soul.*

QUESTION: What are the names of the archangels who work with human karmic records?

According to Rudolf Steiner and other sources, the highest archangels are Michael, Raphael, Gabriel, Uriel, Barakiel, Gamaliel, Pathiel, Meta-tron, Ariel, Chamuel, Japhiel, Raguel, Raziel, Sanaephon, Zadkiel, and Jeremiel.

QUESTION: Can angels change karmic patterns for humans?

They can, but as the Bible states, humans should not pray to angels. Prayers ideally should be directed to God, or to the Creator, who will then "give the angels charge over thee." When prayers are received by angels, they are then evaluated, and answered. In that manner, angels can change or influence a person's karma.

QUESTION: What if prayers are not answered?

They can be repeated fervently. I believe the most-answered prayers are those that are sent out in great desperation or need, or the prayers said for people other than for yourself. There is also the situation where prayers are desperately requested by an individual: according to the works of Elizabeth and Mark Prophet, an angel will be assigned to go before the "Karmic Board," or the seven Lords of Karma, for special consideration.

Prayers of rote, or repetition, are powerful, since they carry the vibration of mass consciousness and great human energy, especially if they are sincere. They are always heard, but are less acknowledged than the simple prayer of a parent for a child.

> You want to live your longest, healthiest life? Find your way, your path. Be in touch with your soul.—Bernie Siegel, M.D.

QUESTION: What questions should we ask ourselves in meditation, for our greatest karmic soul growth?

These are the three most important questions:

1. Why did my soul create this situation?
2. What can I learn from it?
3. What actions do I need to take to correct it?

QUESTION: How can the soul best deal with grief and loss, when the karmic load is unbearably heavy?

Spiritual perspective is the greatest help. On an everyday, mundane level, there is no way that the human mind can, for example, deal with the death of a child. However, if we take the very broad, advanced, metaphysical view, where we have a greater understanding of soul evolution, we will find some solace.

Legitimate spirit communication, where the bereaved understands that "all is well," that love never dies, and that there is still a Great Spirit connection and love, extraordinary healing of the emotions will then occur.

> Life is real! Life is earnest! And the grave is not its goal; dust thou art, to dust returnest, was not spoken of the soul.— Henry Wadsworth Longfellow

QUESTION: How do we know that there is life after death, and that there is such a thing as karma?

There are now thousands of recorded experiences of legitimate near-death experiences (NDEs). By that I mean that many of these experiencers have been able to describe in great detail the moments, and in some cases, hours, after their physical deaths. Many of these people can describe in detail the earthly conversations, environments, and situations that surrounded their physical death. Many books are available on this topic today. From Plato and the early Greeks, through Jesus and Paul, through most African and Asian cultures, to current spiritualists, such as Mme. Helena Blavatsky, a belief in some kind of survival of bodily death has been unequivocally affirmed. Jesus' assertion that His father's house has many mansions would seem to back up this common belief that is held by so many divergent people.

Prophets such as Ezekiel and Isaiah reported powerful spiritual and psychic visions, as does the author of the book of Revelation. In the Gospels, angels speak and Jesus talks with the long-deceased Moses and Elijah (Mt 17:1-3).

QUESTION: If karma is real and life continues after physical death, where are those lives lived? Are they always on the earth?

Once again, I quote from the Bible, wherein Jesus says, "In my father's house are many mansions." This is an indication of the many worlds, and many planes of existence that surround, and include the earth, as great as all infinity, and expansive in a way that is beyond human comprehension. There is "earth karma," but there is also karma that takes humans into many other areas of both physical and non-physical expression.

Our bodies exist on the physical plane, which provides an environment for our activity and growth on Earth and offer us nourishment, stimulation, and joy. There is also a spiritual dimension of the universe that is invisible, and of the spirit world. Our spirit is the internal counterpart to our physical body, and the spirit world is the invisible counterpart to the physical world. This world is located not "up in heaven," but in a different dimension, combining, and inter–penetrating the physical world and the universe. While on Earth, we exist in both worlds simultaneously. Human beings connect the two worlds. This is the reason that people can have visions, extra–sensory perception, and spirit communication. The earth is where worlds collide, hopefully in a good way.

QUESTION: Is celibacy a necessary or important step, toward godliness?

Sex can be a distraction, and can draw one's attention away from godly pursuits, such as meditation and prayer. However, if a person is attempting to be celibate, or live a life free from sensuality, one must be sure that their sex drive is weaker than their desire to "know God." If that is not the case, their energies may need expression, and that particular lifetime may not be suited to celibacy or monastic living. Remember, you have the gift of free will.

QUESTION: Is sex ever a spiritual experience?

If done properly, it should be! (This always gets a laugh.) Our Creator, in addition to the gift of free will, also gave humans the gift of the enjoyment of sex. The sex act should be passionate, loving, gracious, considerate, kind, and appreciative.

QUESTION: Is sex also known as "the fall of man?"

Yes. Sex with the right partner can be joyous and transcendent. Sex with the wrong partner can be base and degrading, and chasing it will keep you mired in the physical for far longer than you need to be. This can last over many lifetimes.

QUESTION: Is birth control ever wrong?

There may have been a time when the earth needed to be populated. That does not seem to be the case any longer. Therefore, birth control, at this point in human evolution, can be beneficial, and is not unspiritual or sinful, as long as it doesn't go against your own beliefs.

QUESTION: Is the formal act of religious "confession" necessary, and does it remove or alleviate karma?

Repeating prayers by rote, without sincerely asking for forgiveness, is quite specious and hollow. An act of anonymous charity might be more effective. Just remember the Akashic, or soul record. It records every thought, word, and deed. What wipes out, or alleviates, bad karma is asking for forgiveness, and then following it up with good, charitable, generous acts of human decency.

QUESTION: Is it karmically or spiritually wrong to eat animals or fish?

The answer is best explained by what Jesus said, "It is not what a man eats that defiles him. It is what he says and does." Eating meat may lower a person's vibrations, and keep that person's energy heavier or denser that is wished; however, humans do have a need for protein, which in some cases, may not be adequate on a vegetarian diet. One must evaluate his or her own physical needs for optimum health and vitality, and also act according to one's own highest spiritual ideal.

QUESTION: Do humans have a "set" time for their physical death?

As it is said in the Bible, "There is a time for every purpose under heaven." However, while the death moment is recorded before one's physical birth, there is great latitude, and flexibility, in almost all cases. The length of time of one's physical life and death may be pre-determined, but can be altered by one's thoughts, words, deeds, actions, and prayers—one's own or others'.

QUESTION: What causes most fears?

Most people experience their greatest fears either from prior incarnation death experiences, which are partially remembered, or in some cases, as a dream or premonition.

QUESTION: Can we die the same way in more than one lifetime?

Rarely. A death experience is repeated if, and when, the lesson was not learned in the prior incarnation. For instance, if a person passed away from a shooting incident, it would not be repeated. That is, unless they are reincarnated, had the desire to have a gun, and took pleasure in killing others.

QUESTION: Is going to the spirit world automatic, or does it depend upon a person's karma?

Yes, it is automatic, and, no, no one is plummeted into hell.

QUESTION: If it is true that God is love, why is there hell?

There is only hell for those who expect it, and even that is very brief, and never necessary. In the case of a person such as Hitler, when they cross over, there is usually a long resting time, purification, and then the opportunity for his soul's restitution, along with the healing of others who are in need.

QUESTION: Does it matter what we are wearing, or what we look like when we die?

No, because even with cremation, there is a glorious spirit body that is the true essence of the soul. That is what will cloak all humans after physical passing.

QUESTION: What do people do in the spirit world?

There is much work to be done, if one wishes to do it. There are spirit greeters, for example, who help to greet and guide those who have just crossed over. There are spirit schools, with many levels of teaching and learning. There is spirit/human interaction, where those in physical incarnations receive "inspiration," comfort, teachings, dreams, and direction. There is usually no physical sex or eating of animals or fish. However, there are many joyful experiences, which include music, dancing, and angelic interaction. There is as much to do, or not to do, as one wishes. There is the great joy of out–of–body travel, which includes going to many other, vast, unimaginable planes and dimensions. It is always acknowledged that coming into an earthly body is, in its own way, amazing and terrific, but can be rather confining . . . especially after the experience of cosmic travel to other worlds.

QUESTION: Is religion important to our karmic expression?

Religion is important when it succeeds in connecting a person to the God within, through meditation, prayer, and service. If religion fails to connect a person with their true, God–like spiritual heritage, it is a failure as a religion.

QUESTION: Will we meet God after we die? Does it depend upon our karma?

Yes. God is love, God is light. God is all. After physical death, one goes into the Clear Light, which is the essence of God, or the Creator. God is the end–all, the be–all, and the ultimate bliss.

GOD BLESS YOU.

Appendix

For Easy Reference

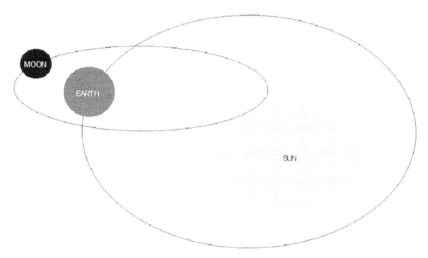

THE NODES CHART
Past Life = South Node, Destiny = North Node

(1)

Past Life—Gemini, Destiny—Sagittarius
Jan. 1, 1900–Dec. 28, 1900
January 20, 1918–August 9, 1919
September 2, 1936–March 21, 1938
April 13, 1955–November 4, 1956
Nov. 23, 1973–June 12, 1975
July 5, 1992–January 21, 1994

(2)

Past Life—Taurus, Destiny—Scorpio
Dec. 29, 1901–July 17, 1902
August 10, 1919–February 26, 1921
March 22, 1938–October 9, 1939
Nov. 5, 1956–May 21, 1958

June 13, 1975–December 29, 1976
January 22, 1994–August 11, 1995

(3)
Past Life—Aries, Destiny—Libra
July 18, 1902–February 4, 1904
February 27, 1921–September 15, 1922
October 10, 1939–April 27, 1941
May 22, 1958–December 8, 1959
November 29, 1928–June 18, 1930
August 12, 1995–February 27, 1997

(4)
Past Life—Pisces, Destiny—Virgo
February 5, 1904–August 23, 1905
September 16, 1922–April 4, 1924
April 28, 1941–November 15, 1942
December 9, 1959–July 3, 1961
July 20, 1978–February 5, 1980
February 28, 1997–September 17, 1998

(5)
Past Life—Aquarius, Destiny—Leo
August 24, 1905–March 13, 1907
April 5, 1924–October 22, 1925
November 16, 1942–June 3, 1944
July 4, 1961–January 13, 1963
February 6, 1980–August 25, 1981
September 18, 1998–April 5, 2000

(6)
Past Life—Capricorn, Destiny—Cancer
March 14, 1907–September 29, 1908
October 23, 1925–May 12, 1927
June 4, 1944–December 23, 1945
January 14, 1963–August 5, 1964
August 26, 1981–March 14, 1983

April 6, 2000–October 12, 2001

(7)

Past Life—Sagittarius, Destiny—Gemini
September 30, 1908–April 18, 1910
May 13, 1927–November 28, 1928
December 24, 1945–July 11, 1947
March 15, 1983–October 1, 1984
August 6, 1964–February 21, 1966

(8)

Past Life—Scorpio, Destiny—Taurus
April 19, 1910–November 7, 1911
November 29, 1928–June 18, 1930
July 12, 1947–January 28, 1949
February 22, 1966–September 9, 1967
October 2, 1984–April 20, 1986

(9)

Past Life—Libra, Destiny—Aries
November 8, 1911–May 26, 1913
June 19, 1930–January 6, 1932
January 29, 1949–August 17, 1950
September 10, 1967–March 28, 1969
April 21, 1986–November 8, 1987

(10)

Past Life—Virgo, Destiny—Pisces
May 27, 1913–December 13, 1914
January 7, 1932–July 25, 1933
August 18, 1950–March 7, 1952
March 29, 1969–October 15, 1970
November 9, 1987–May 28, 1989

(11)

Past Life—Leo, Destiny—Aquarius
December 14, 1914–July 2, 1916

172 Why Am I Here?

July 26, 1933–February 12, 1935
March 8, 1952–October 2, 1953
October 16, 1970–May 5, 1972
May 29, 1989–December 15, 1990

(12)
Past Life—Cancer, Destiny—Capricorn
July 3, 1916–January 19, 1918
February 13, 1935–September 1, 1926
October 3, 1953–April 12, 1955
May 6, 1972–November 22, 1973
December 16, 1990–July 4, 1992

Life Lessons

BIRTH, CONCEPTION AND FAMILIES

Hatred for, or lack of identity with, one's parents.
LESSON: forgiveness, learning to love one another.

Abortion, as an incoming fetus.
LESSON: flexibility.

Abortion, as a parent.
LESSON: trust in God's plan, selflessness and discernment.

Miscarriage, Stillbirth.
LESSON for parents: faith in knowing there is a universal reason for everything and all will be taken care of in God's time.

Crib Death.
LESSON for parents: faith, there is a reason for everything.

Infertility.
LESSON: reverence towards the Creator and all things Divine, "There is a time for everything under heaven."

Adoption, for the child.
LESSON: adjustment, appreciation, forgiveness, to overcome feelings of rejection by loving and receiving love.

Adoption, for the birth parents.
LESSON: overcome ego, love unconditionally.

Fertile Abundance.
LESSON: trust, discernment, selflessness and faith.

Multiple birth siblings.
LESSON: sharing, developing identity, selflessness.

HOW WE ARE PERCEIVED

Shy, Gawky, Unattractive.
LESSON: Stand tall, breathe deeply, adopt courage and an aura of success, walking the road as a free and confident being.

Physical Shortcomings or Handicaps.
LESSON: Balance. Develop your spiritual potential. Respect others and they will respect you and bolster your self-esteem to the point where, with effort, you will accomplish marvelous things.

Obesity or Other Weight Issues.
LESSON: Know that you have all that you need now, and that the Universal Creator will provide.

Self-Importance.
LESSON: Take interest in others. Ask them about themselves, their work, their interests. Remember we are all equally children of God in our immortal soul state.

Fear of Putting Yourself out There.
LESSON: Go out for a walk and breathe the fresh air deeply. Smile at everyone you pass and be amazed at the smiles you get back. Show enthusiasm and sociability for all and receive the same back. You might just change the life of someone who was just like you.

LOVE, SEX AND RELATIONSHIPS

Inability to give or receive love.
LESSON: As the Master said, "Love one another as I have loved you."

Loyalty, Fidelity, Monogamy.
LESSON: Reap what you have sown.

Infidelity, Immaturity in relationships, Inability to commit.

LESSON: The person you are with is the one you are meant to be with at this point in time.
Sexual Dysfunction.
LESSON: Patience, effort, forbearance.

Inflicting Spousal Abuse.
LESSON: Harm, especially on those weaker than yourself, will be re-enacted tenfold. Learn selfless love and respect for others, as well as yourself.

Accepting Spousal Abuse.
LESSON: self-worth, allowing others to do harm is not a substitute for love.

Overt Kinkiness/Promiscuity.
LESSON: Self-worth and self-love.

Emotional Conditions and Their Lessons

ANGER/HOSTILITY

"He that is slow to anger is better than the mighty; and he that ruleth his spirit better than he that taketh a city." (Proverbs 16:32) Anger is one of the most destructive influences of and on the mind.

LESSON: Control, love and empathy.

CONDEMNATION

A double-edged sword, highly destructive. "Let he who is without fault cast the first stone." (John 8:7) Recognize your own flaws, only when you are perfect may you move on to others.

LESSON: Love and recognize the unconditional worth of others.

CRITICAL DESTRUCTIVENESS

It is the inferior person who needs to be superior to others.

LESSON: Recognize worth in others.

DECEIT

Deceit rebounds with self-condemnation and lack of self-esteem. It results in imbalances of body and mind.

LESSON: Love yourself and others enough to not deceive them.

HYPOCRISY

Physiological ills are often a direct result of guilt and cloaked behavior. Guilt can kill you.

LESSON: Truthfulness in all things.

FEAR

Mankind's enemy, the root of many problems. Excise it from your soul.

LESSON: Stimulus to action.

GREED/ACQUISITIVENESS

Jesus asked, "What would it profit you to gain the whole world and lose your own soul?" Spiritual growth is more valuable than all the material possessions we might acquire.

LESSON: Realignment of values.

HATRED
Look for the underlying fear then excise it. Do not cast your negative emotions upon others; they have the same right to learn as you do even if they have caused you great harm. Replace hatred with a desire to find the God Power within the persons we despise. Hatred engenders hatred, love begets love.
LESSON: Forgiveness, trust, unselfish love.

HOPELESSNESS
There is no chance; rather, there is a divine nature to all things. Everything happens so that we may move upward in the eternal progress of life.
LESSON: Trust.

HYPERSENSITIVITY
Having to do with an individual's sense of importance and wounded pride.
LESSON: Offense at any slight is a negative impulse, real or imagined.

IMPATIENCE
Indiscriminate action breeds fear, discouragement, irritability, and ultimately self-condemnation.
LESSON: Tolerance, action and faith.

INABILITY TO GIVE OR RECEIVE LOVE
Love is the most powerful spiritual force in the universe, expressing the greatest qualities of the soul. True love, which comes from the Creator, is untainted by jealousy, possession, lack of trust, or selfishness. This lack is often caused by repeat disappointments in love, or growing up in an environment with little loving expression.
LESSON: As the Master said, "Love one another as I have loved you." (John 15:12)

IRRITABILITY
A subtle form of anger which over a period of time is capable of harm to the physical body.
LESSON: There are choices in life; stay rational.

JEALOUSY
Highly negative impulse causing harm to yourself and others.
LESSON: Trust in others and in infinite wisdom.

LACK OF ASPIRATION
Lack of hope or slipping backwards, in reality or in one's mind.
LESSON: Openness to new promise or ideals.

LACK OF COURAGE
Caused by disappointment, belief in one's failure.
LESSON: Loyalty, devotion and commitment.

LACK OF EMPATHY
Deference to the distress and suffering of others is vital in the soul's growth.
LESSON: We are our brothers' keepers.

LACK OF FAITH
Would you go on a car trip without a road map? Lack of faith is caused by disappointment and discouragement, when it becomes part of one's personality it can result in bitterness and confusion and ultimately, in grave physical imbalances. There is order in the universe, disaster on the face of it may look like disaster but there is often an underlying spiritual cause, a higher lesson to be learned, and a place to go from there. If you despair not, your pain will come to an end.
LESSON: Trust in the divine nature of things.

LACK OF FORGIVENESS
"Forgive them father, they know not what they do," said Jesus. (Luke 23:34) The inability to forgive one's self or others clutches negativity to the heart, usually resulting in illness in the physical body.
LESSON: Universal love.

LACK OF KINDNESS
Rise above greed, hatred, jealousy or envy.
LESSON: We feel less sorry for ourselves when we respond to the needs of others.

PREJUDICE/INTOLERANCE
Dwelling on insignificant details or petty annoyances is the opposite of genuine understanding. "Judge not, lest ye yourself be judged." (Matthew 7:1)
LESSON: You are falling backwards on the path to soul growth and enlightenment.

PRIDE/BOASTFULNESS/SELF–CENTEREDNESS
Qualities which retard the development of the soul.
LESSON: Recognize worth in others, not be so quick to boast about your own.

SELF–CONDEMNATION
Another worthless emotion, unless it is followed with a plan for not repeating past mistakes.
LESSON: Love yourself, forgive.

SELFISHNESS
The opposite of kindness and generosity, a form of self–protection, of fear. : "And though I have the gift of prophecy and understand all the mysteries, and all the knowledge; and though I have all faith, so that I could remove mountains, and have not charity, I have nothing." (1 Corinthians 13:2) Truly, we must do unto others as we would have them do unto us.
LESSON: "Bread cast upon the waters will be returned threefold in time."

VANITY
The need for recognition and approval.
LESSON: Self–worth comes from inside.

WORRY
A worried, troubled mind causes illness to manifest in the body. Worry accomplishes nothing.
LESSON: Positive action.

About the Authors

JOYCE KELLER has been honored in Simon and Schuster's, *Top 100 Psychics in America*, as well as many issues of *Who's Who*, and has appeared on major TV talk shows. A columnist at LifetimeTV.com for more than fifteen years, Joyce is the author of seven international best-selling books, and endorsed by Regis Philbin.

Keller's books include *Calling All Angels*, *The Complete Book of Numerology*, and *Seven Steps to Heaven: How to Communicate with Those We've Loved and Lost*. She has also written the best-selling, "Micro Mag Books for American Media," entitled, *Your Angel Astrology Love Diet*, *An Astrology Guide to Your Guardian Angels*, and *Your Angel Astrology Guide to Health and Healing*. These books have sold in the millions.

Keller is a Certified Hypnotherapist, specializing in past-life regression, and past-life issues, such as weight control.

Keller hosts one of America's longest-running live, advice, AM/FM and web radio programs, "The Joyce Keller Show," on BlogTalkRadio.com/joyce-keller, as well as through her website, at www.JoyceKeller.com, where she interacts with listeners located throughout the world.

ELAINE J. KELLER, Co-Author

Elaine J. Keller is an author, illustrator, and editor living in Brooklyn, N.Y. Her books include *Working in Commercials*; the novel *A Covenant of Poppies*; *A Mother's New World Order Handbook*; *Light Your Fire*; *Ayurveda for Weight Loss*; and *Tale of Running Bear* (Author/Illustrator). Keller's short fiction has appeared in such publications as *The Commonline Journal*, *The Rusty Nail*, and *Nazar-Look Magazine*. She is a recipient of a state grant for writing, a member of the Author's Guild, and a graduate of NYU. See more at www.elainejkeller.com

Bibliography

Cerminara, Gina. *Many Mansions: The Edgar Cayce Story of Reincarnation.* New York, NY: Signet, 1988.

Chamberlain, David, M.D. *Babies Remember Birth.* New York, NY: Ballantine Books, 1989.

Fisher, Joe. *The Case for Reincarnation.* New York, NY: Bantam, 1985.

Goodman, Linda. *Sun Signs.* New York, NY: Bantam, Reissue edition, 1985.

Guiley, Rosemary E. *Harper's Encyclopedia of Mystical and Paranormal Experience.* New York, NY: Book Sales, 2nd edition, 1994.

MacLaine, Shirley. *Out on a Limb.* New York, NY: Bantam, 1986.

Peele, Stanton, and Archie Brodsky. *Love and Addiction.* Broadrow, 2015.

Prophet, Mark. *The Answer You're Looking for Is Inside of You.* Gardiner, MT: Summit University, 1997.

Subramuniyaswami, Sivaya. *Dancing with Siva.* Kapaa, HI: Himalayan Academy Publications, 1997.

Yogananda, Paramahansa. *Autobiography of a Yogi.* London, UK: Rider, 1955.

4TH DIMENSION PRESS

An Imprint of A.R.E. Press

4th Dimension Press is an imprint of A.R.E. Press, the publishing division of Edgar Cayce's Association for Research and Enlightenment (A.R.E.).

We publish books, DVDs, and CDs in the fields of intuition, psychic abilities, ancient mysteries, philosophy, comparative religious studies, personal and spiritual development, and holistic health.

For more information, or to receive a catalog, contact us by mail, phone, or online at:

4th Dimension Press
215 67th Street
Virginia Beach, VA 23451-2061
800-333-4499

4THDIMENSIONPRESS.COM

Who Was Edgar Cayce?
Twentieth Century Psychic and Medical Clairvoyant

Edgar Cayce (pronounced Kay-Cee, 1877-1945) has been called the "sleeping prophet," the "father of holistic medicine," and the most-documented psychic of the 20th century. For more than 40 years of his adult life, Cayce gave psychic "readings" to thousands of seekers while in an unconscious state, diagnosing illnesses and revealing lives lived in the past and prophecies yet to come. But who, exactly, was Edgar Cayce?

Cayce was born on a farm in Hopkinsville, Kentucky, in 1877, and his psychic abilities began to appear as early as his childhood. He was able to see and talk to his late grandfather's spirit, and often played with "imaginary friends" whom he said were spirits on the other side. He also displayed an uncanny ability to memorize the pages of a book simply by sleeping on it. These gifts labeled the young Cayce as strange, but all Cayce really wanted was to help others, especially children.

Later in life, Cayce would find that he had the ability to put himself into a sleep-like state by lying down on a couch, closing his eyes, and folding his hands over his stomach. In this state of relaxation and meditation, he was able to place his mind in contact with all time and space—the universal consciousness, also known as the super-conscious mind. From there, he could respond to questions as broad as, "What are the secrets of the universe?" and "What is my purpose in life?" to as specific as, "What can I do to help my arthritis?" and "How were the pyramids of Egypt built?" His responses to these questions came to be called "readings," and their insights offer practical help and advice to individuals even today.

The majority of Edgar Cayce's readings deal with holistic health and the treatment of illness. Yet, although best known for this material, the sleeping Cayce did not seem to be limited to concerns about the physical body. In fact, in their entirety, the readings discuss an astonishing 10,000 different topics. This vast array of subject matter can be narrowed down into a smaller group of topics that, when compiled together, deal with the following five categories: (1) Health-Related Information; (2) Philosophy and Reincarnation; (3) Dreams and Dream Interpretation; (4) ESP and Psychic Phenomena; and (5) Spiritual Growth, Meditation, and Prayer.

Learn more at EdgarCayce.org.

What Is A.R.E.?

Edgar Cayce founded the non-profit Association for Research and Enlightenment (A.R.E.) in 1931, to explore spirituality, holistic health, intuition, dream interpretation, psychic development, reincarnation, and ancient mysteries—all subjects that frequently came up in the more than 14,000 documented psychic readings given by Cayce.

The Mission of the A.R.E. is to help people transform their lives for the better, through research, education, and application of core concepts found in the Edgar Cayce readings and kindred materials that seek to manifest the love of God and all people and promote the purposefulness of life, the oneness of God, the spiritual nature of humankind, and the connection of body, mind, and spirit.

With an international headquarters in Virginia Beach, Va., a regional headquarters in Houston, regional representatives throughout the U.S., Edgar Cayce Centers in more than thirty countries, and individual members in more than seventy countries, the A.R.E. community is a global network of individuals.

A.R.E. conferences, international tours, camps for children and adults, regional activities, and study groups allow like-minded people to gather for educational and fellowship opportunities worldwide.

A.R.E. offers membership benefits and services that include a quarterly body-mind-spirit member magazine, Venture Inward, a member newsletter covering the major topics of the readings, and access to the entire set of readings in an exclusive online database.

Learn more at EdgarCayce.org.

EDGARCAYCE.ORG